Classical Guitar

ANTHOLOGY

32 Classical Masterpieces Arranged for Solo Guitar

By Bridget Mermikides

To access audio visit:
www.halleonard.com/mylibrary

Enter Code
1805-5957-3306-4343

ISBN 978-1-4950-4625-4

7777 W. BLUEMOUND RD. P.O. BOX 13819 MILWAUKEE, WI 53213

In Australia Contact:
Hal Leonard Australia Pty. Ltd.
4 Lentara Court
Cheltenham, Victoria, 3192 Australia
Email: ausadmin@halleonard.com.au

Visit Hal Leonard Online at
www.halleonard.com

I dedicate this book to my late mother Mary Upson,
who would have loved listening to these pieces.

All arrangements and performances by Bridget Mermikides.
Audio production and engineering by Milton Mermikides.

Contents

Introduction

Many thanks for purchasing the *Classical Guitar Anthology*. The positive response to my first book of arrangements *The Classical Guitar Compendium* has been hugely appreciated, and I am indebted to Hal Leonard and the many guitarists from around the world for their continued support.

This book represents a substantial amount of work bringing a diverse set of beautiful and timeless pieces to the classical guitar. I've worked hard to preserve the sentiment and musical content of the original works, while making them enjoyable to play and listen to. As a result there is a wide range of technical challenges here, and some of these may need significant investment, but are well worth the effort.

In addition to my arrangements I have included two pieces – the only ones here originally written for guitar – by Francisco Tárrega, which are a lovely addition to any repertoire.

Also included are downloadable recordings of me playing every one of these arrangements, which you may find useful while learning the pieces, or deciding what to learn next.

Enjoy,

Bridget

Asturias-Leyenda
Suite Espanola No. 5

Isaac Albéniz
Arranged by Bridget Mermikides

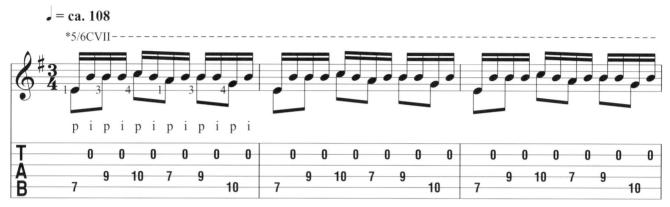

*4th & 5th strings only.

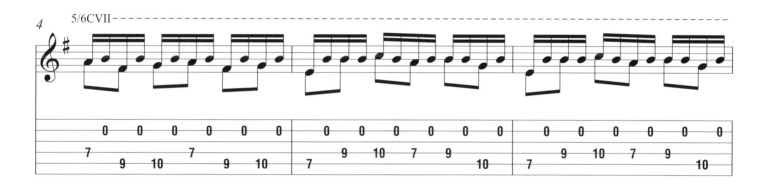

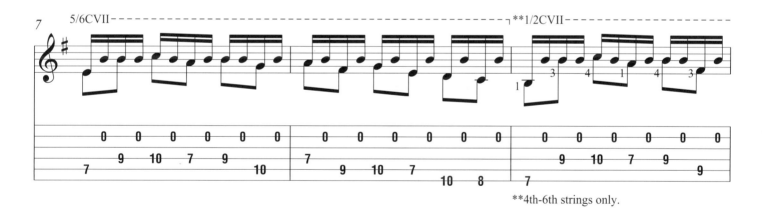

**4th-6th strings only.

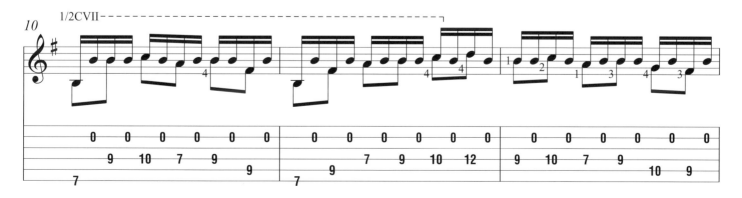

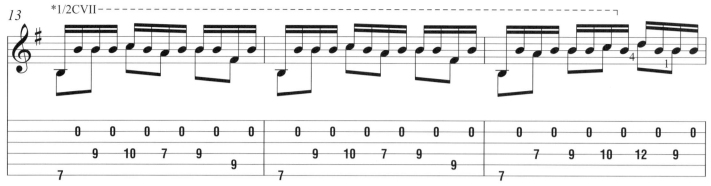

*4th-6th strings only.

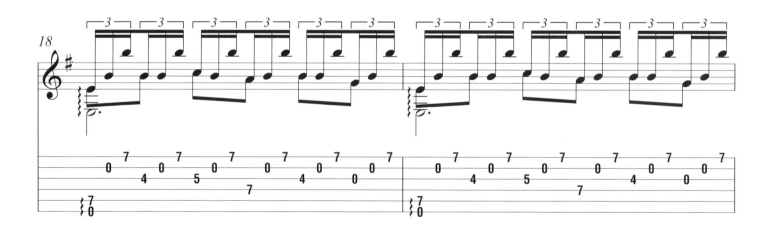

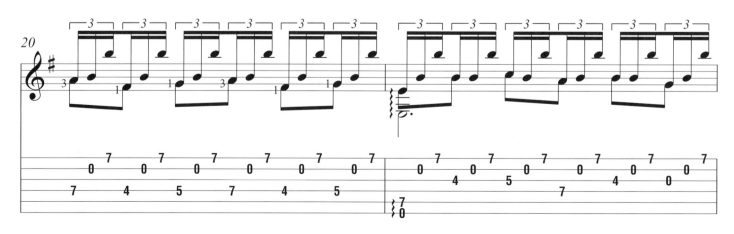

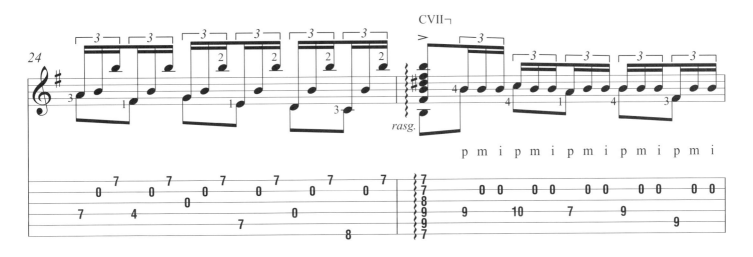

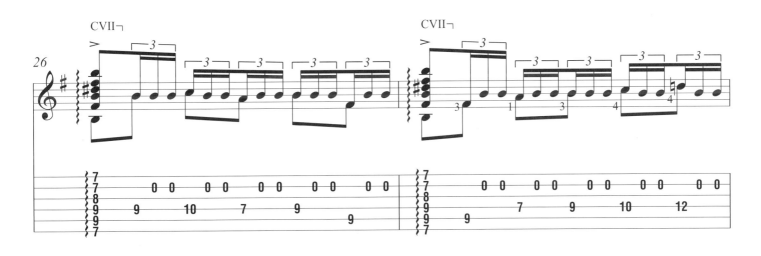

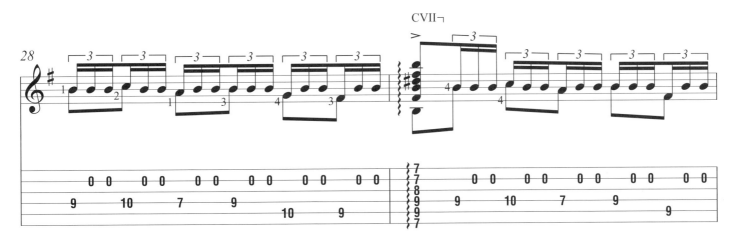

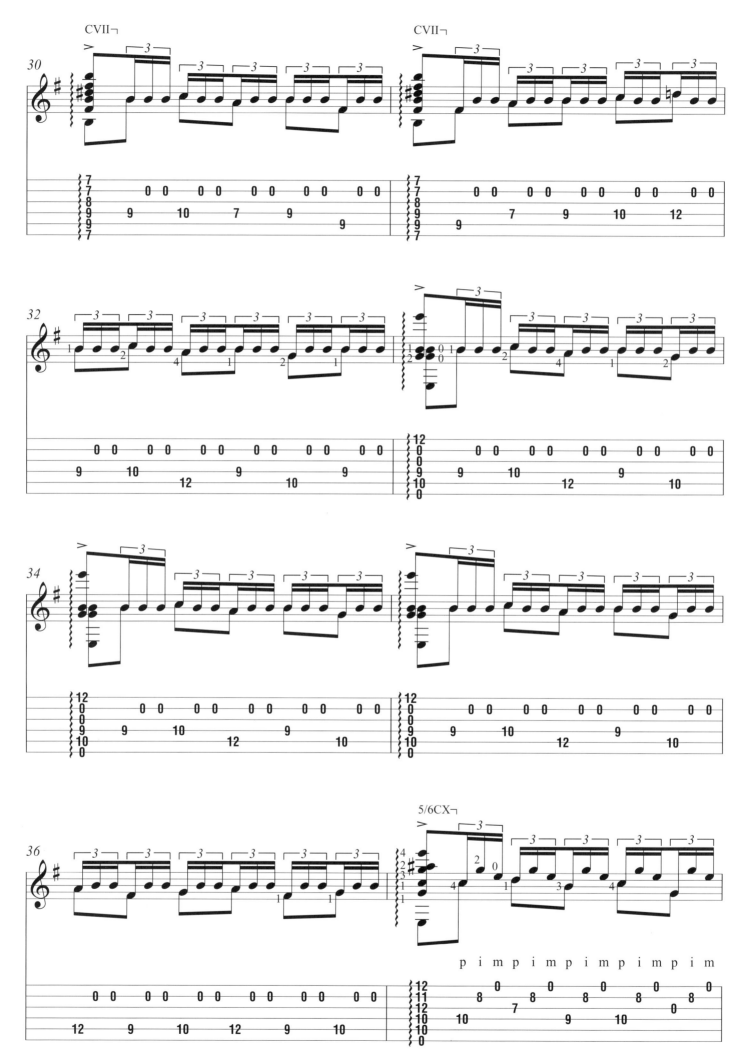

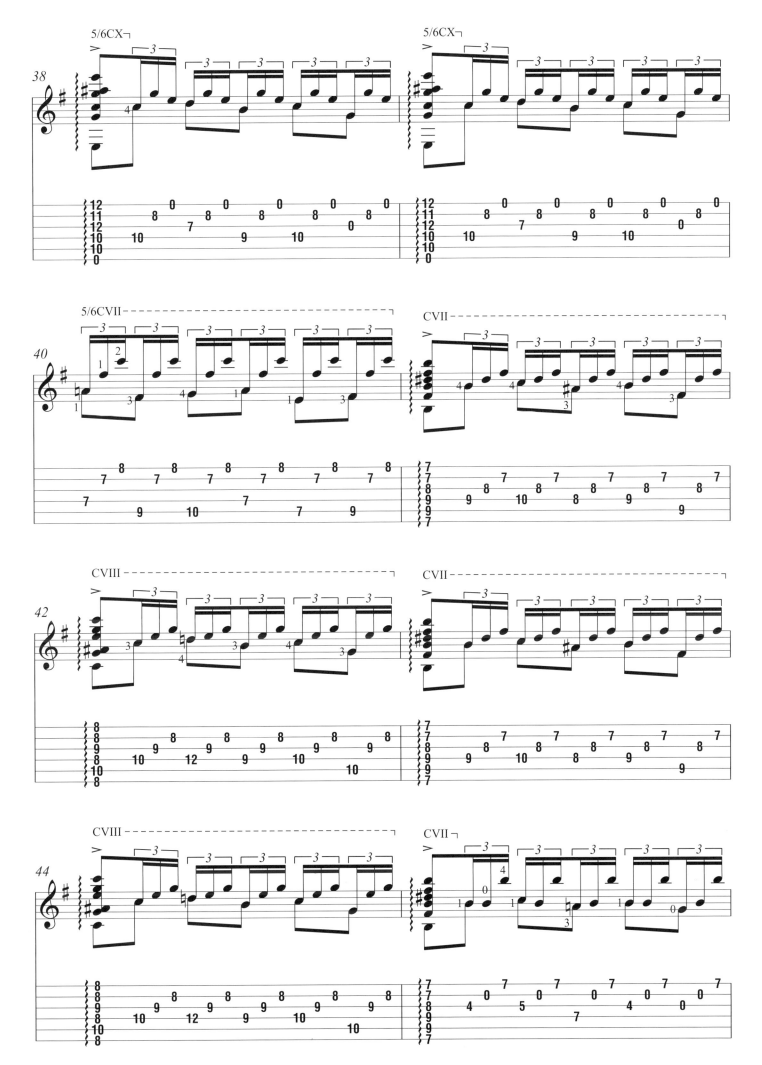

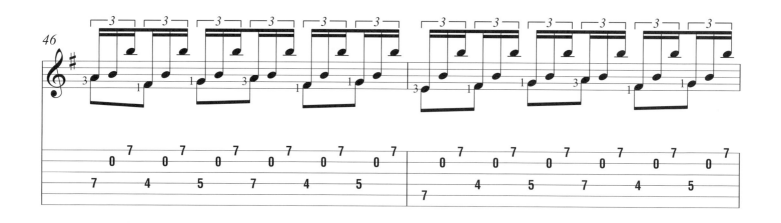

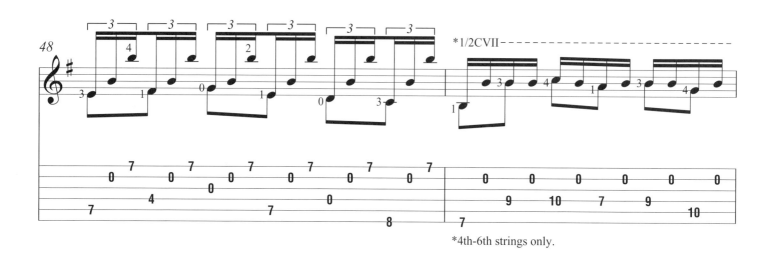

*4th-6th strings only.

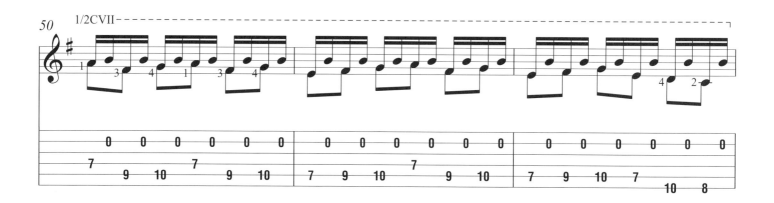

To Coda ⊕

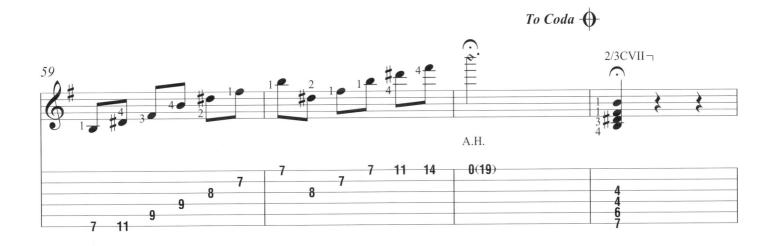

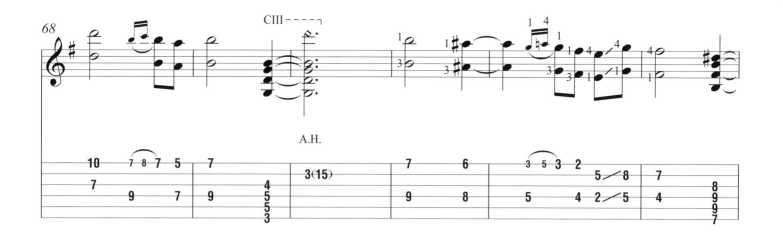

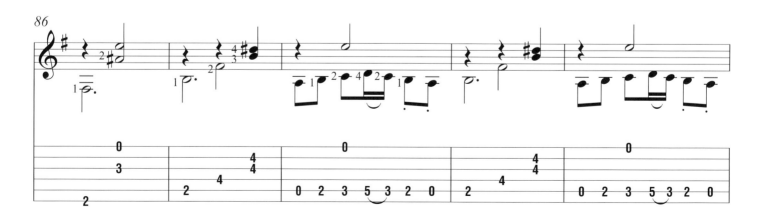

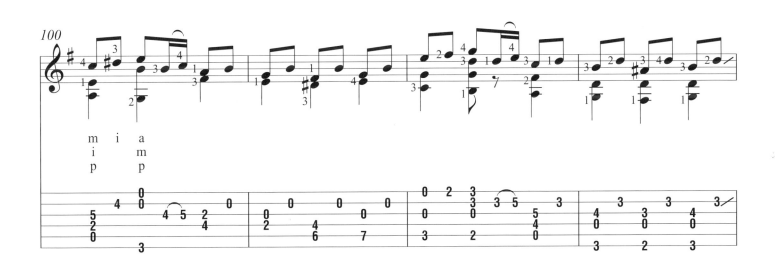

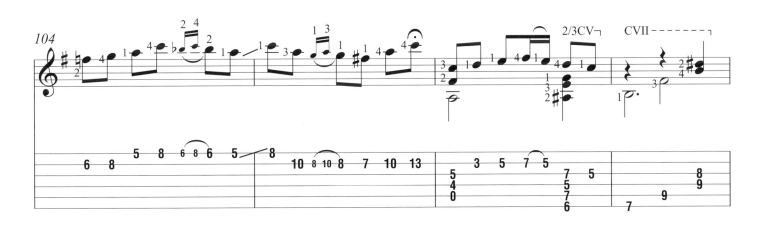

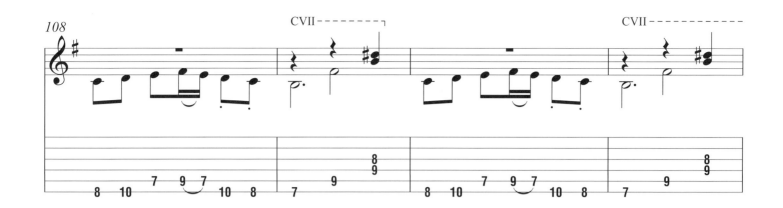

D.C. al Coda

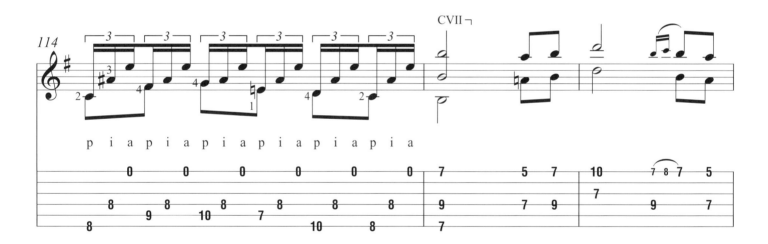

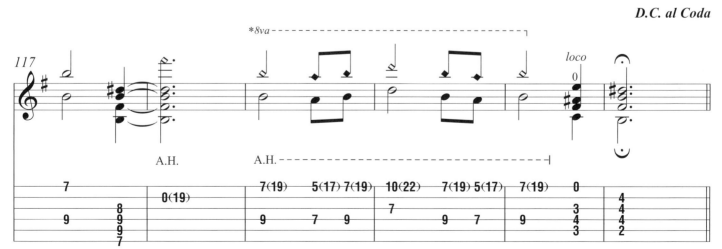

*Applies to upstemmed notes only.

⊕ Coda

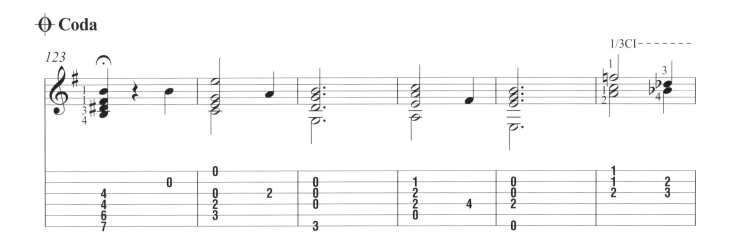

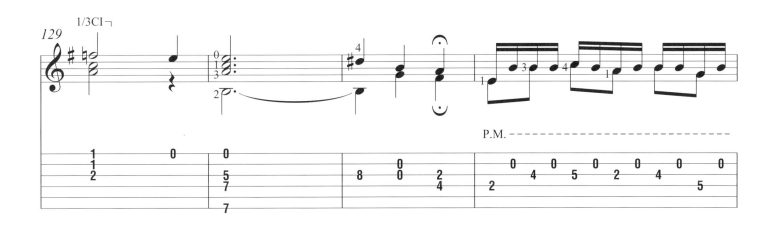

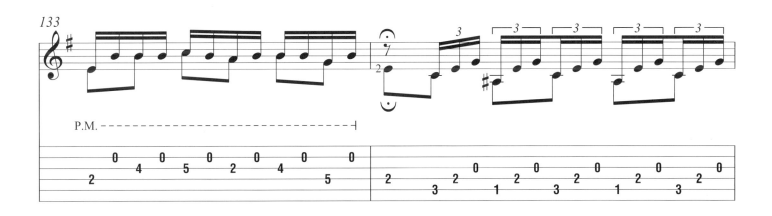

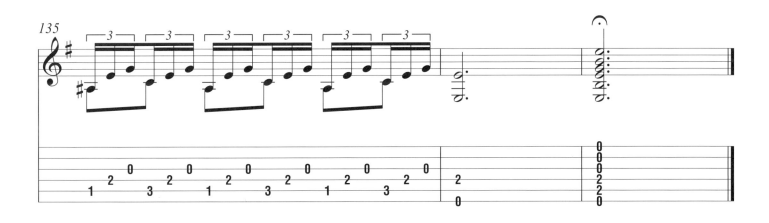

Granada

Isaac Albéniz
Arranged by Bridget Mermikides

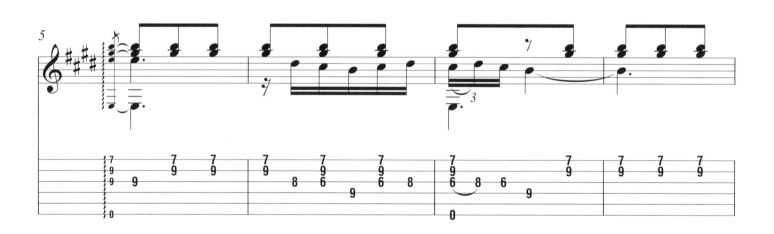

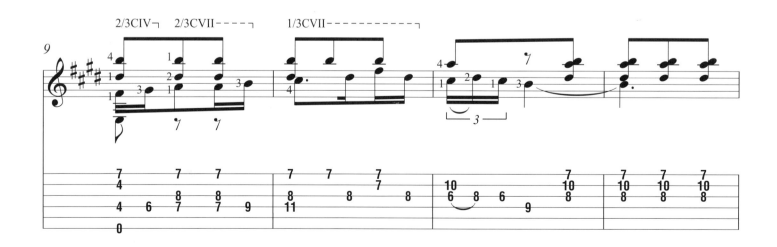

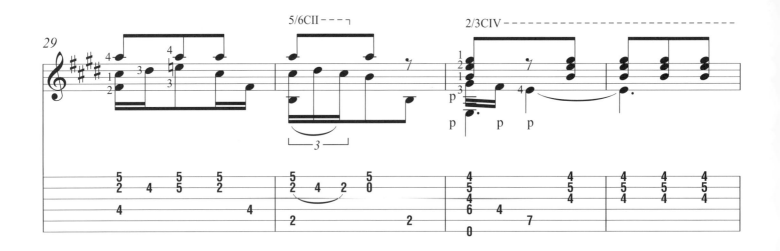

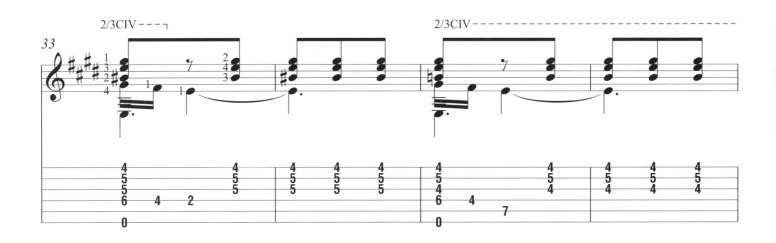

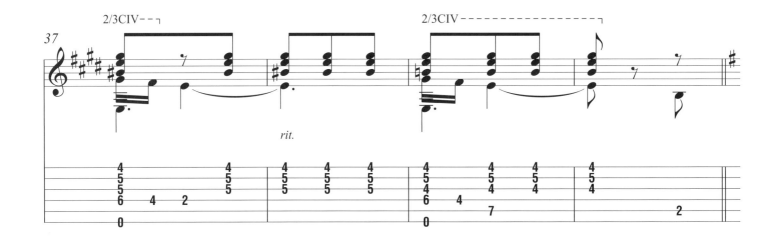

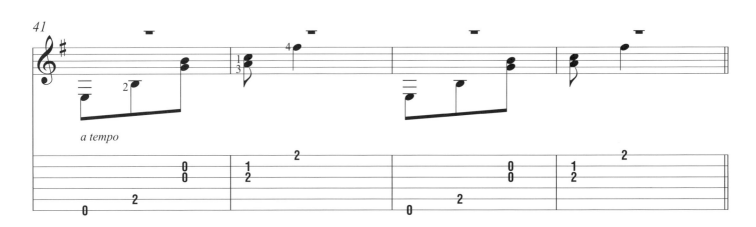

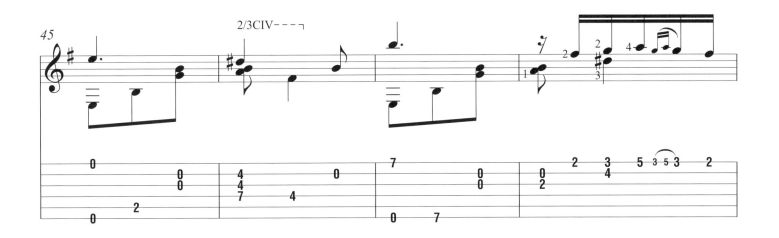

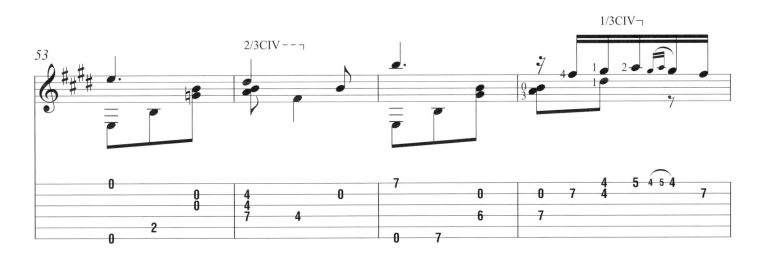

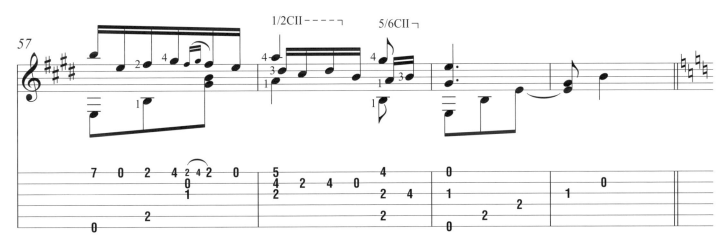

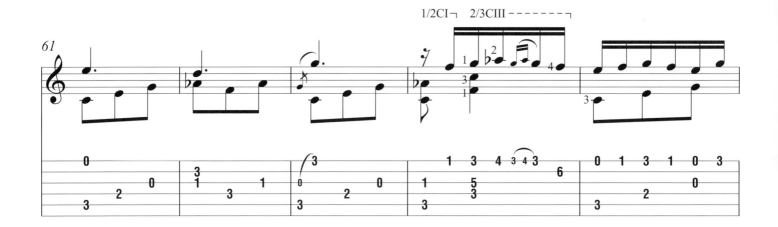

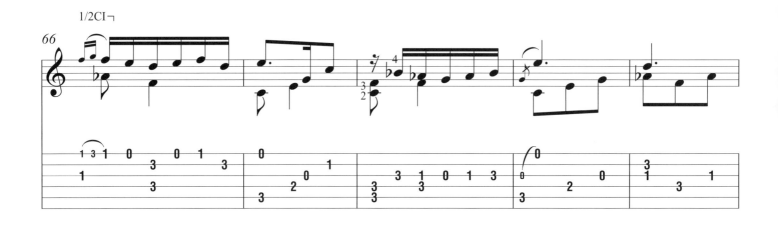

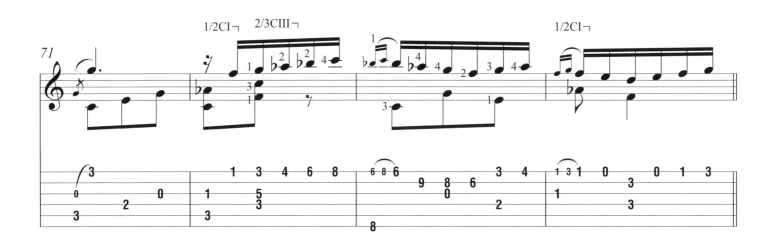

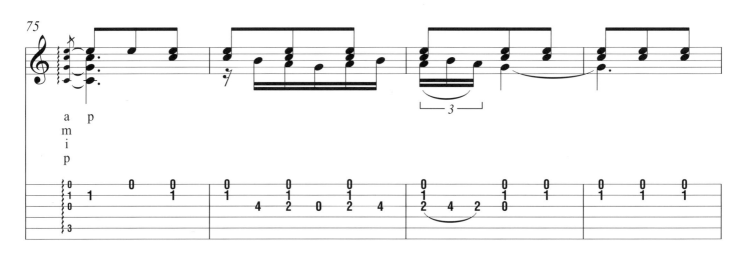

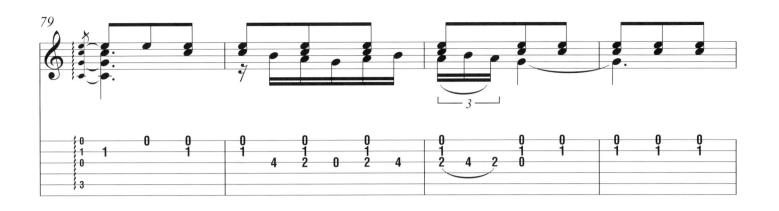

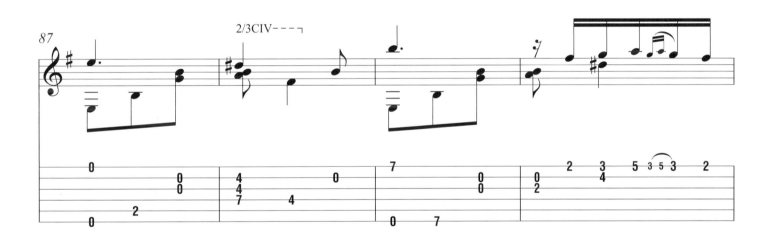

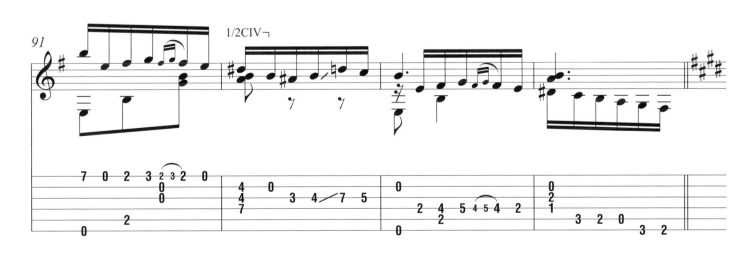

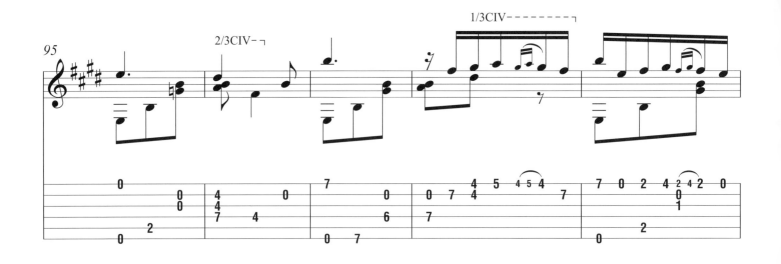

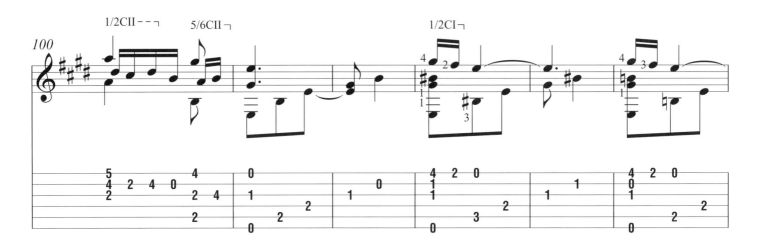

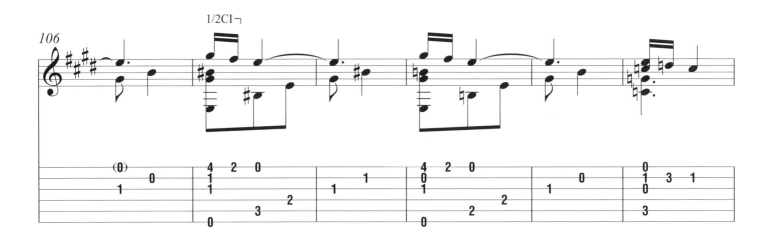

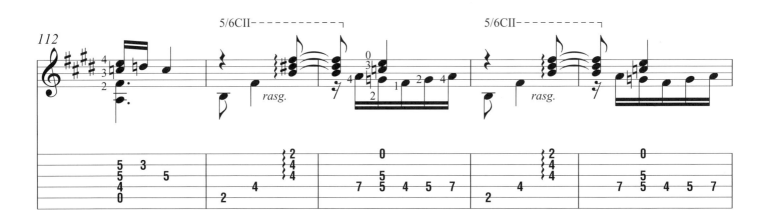

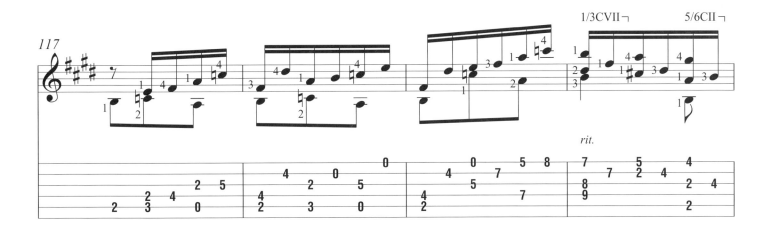

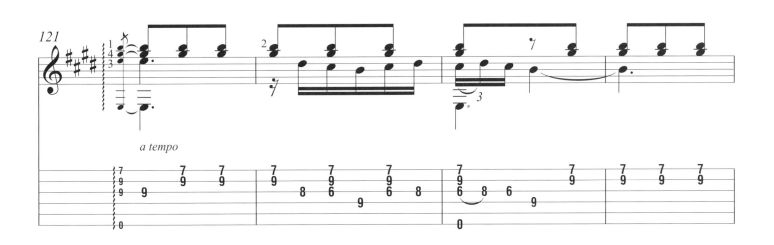

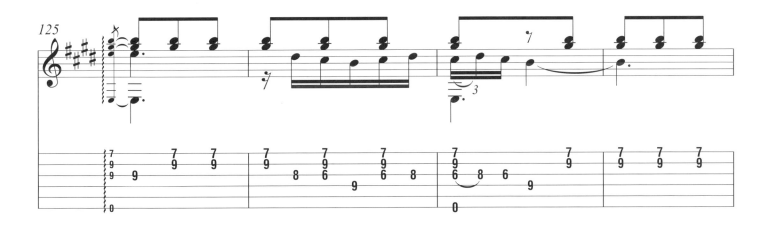

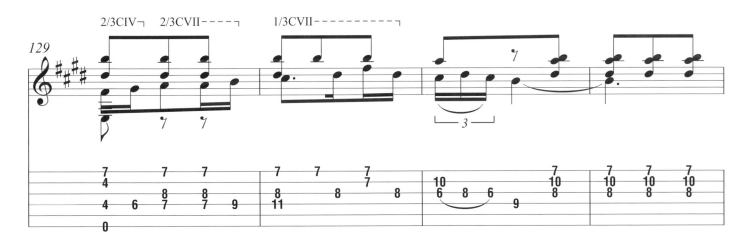

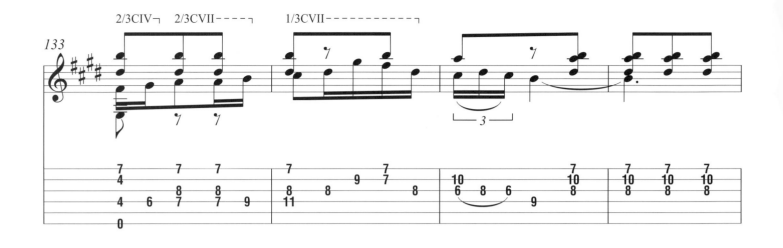

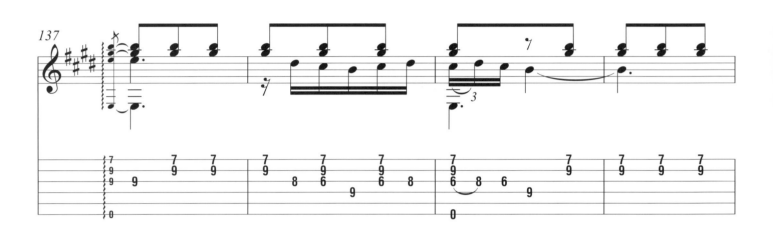

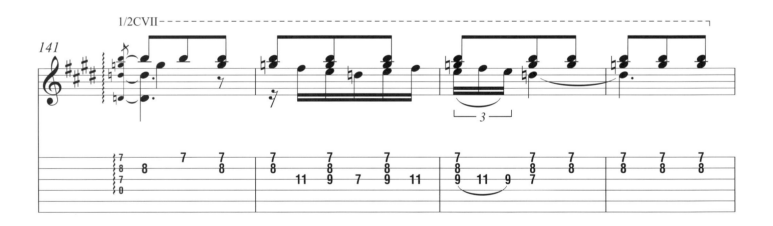

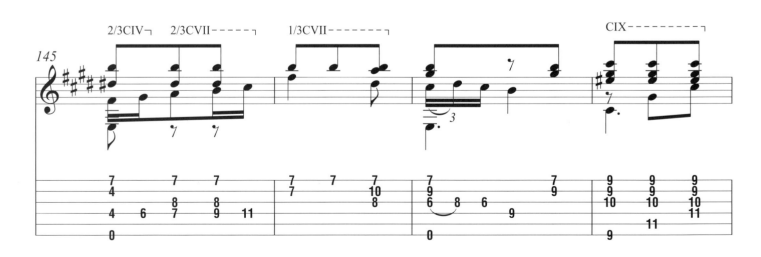

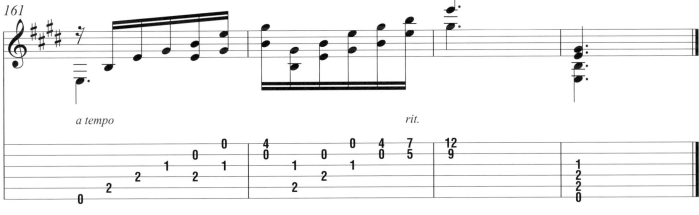

Tango in D, Op. 165, No. 2

Isaac Albéniz
Arranged by Bridget Mermikides

Drop D tuning:
(low to high) D-A-D-G-B-E

♩ = ca. 45

Harm.

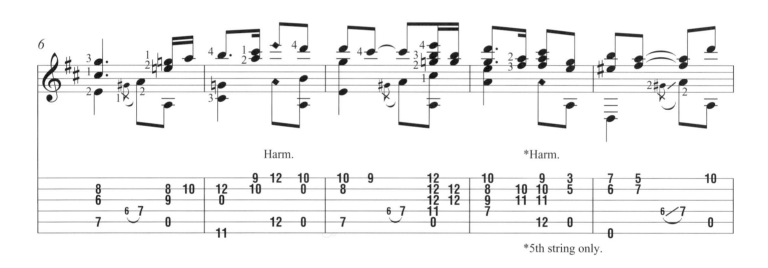

Harm.   *Harm.

*5th string only.

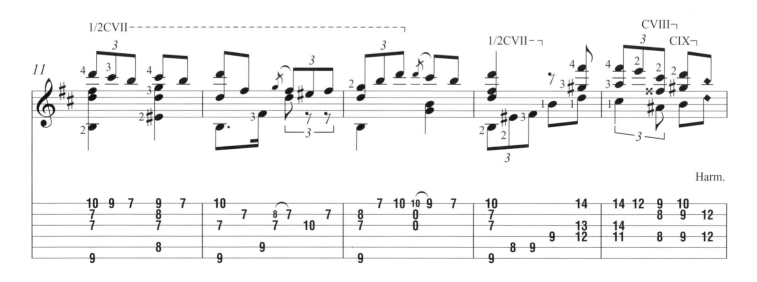

Harm.

*Harm.

*5th string only.

Arioso from Cantata, BWV 156

Johann Sebastian Bach
Arranged by Bridget Mermikides

Drop D tuning:
(low to high) D-A-D-G-B-E

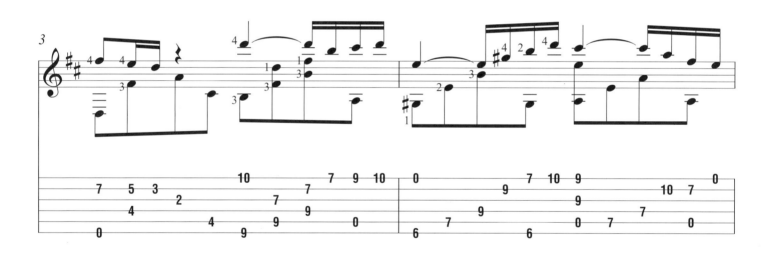

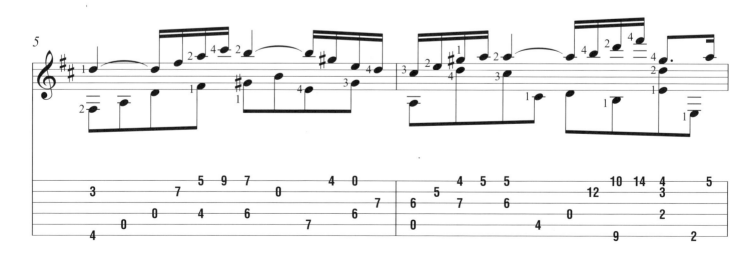

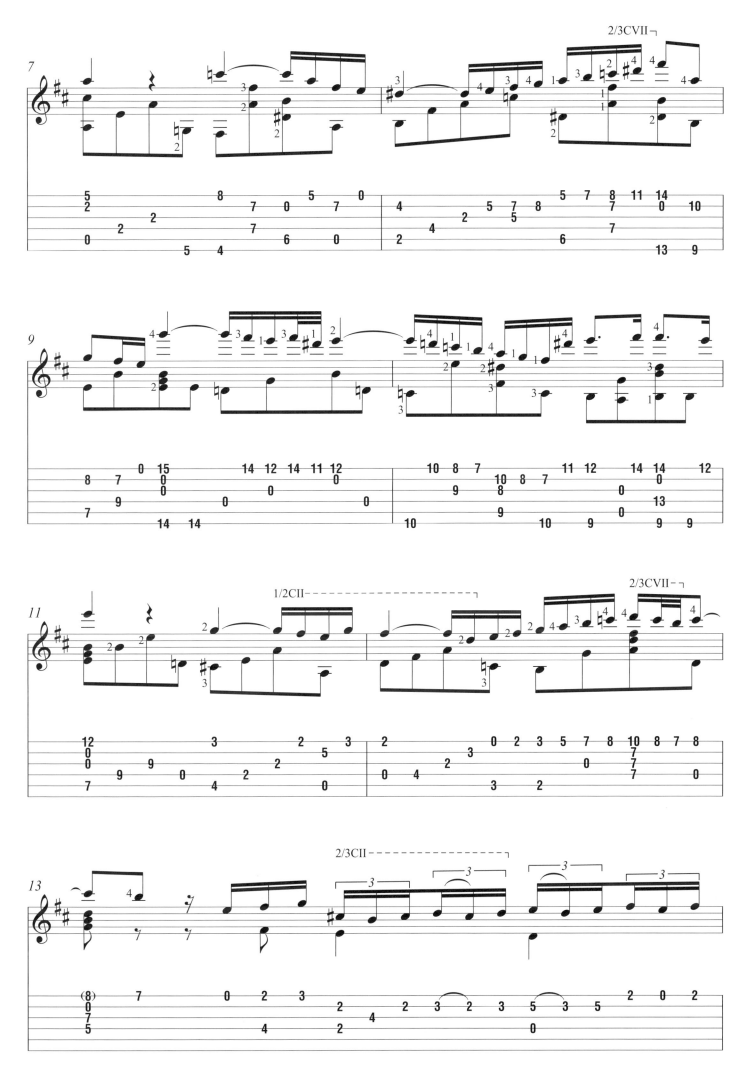

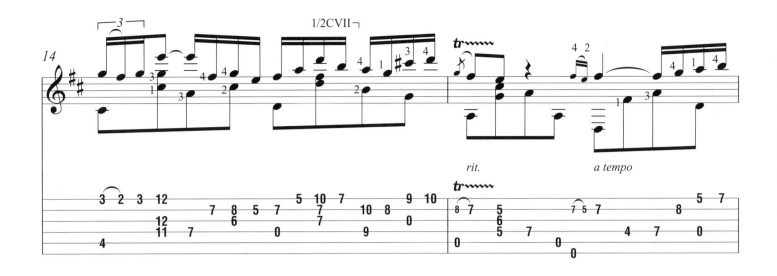

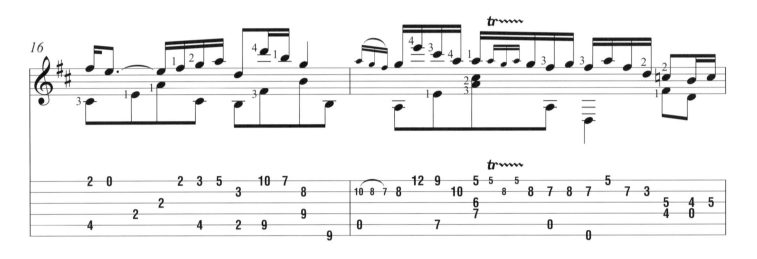

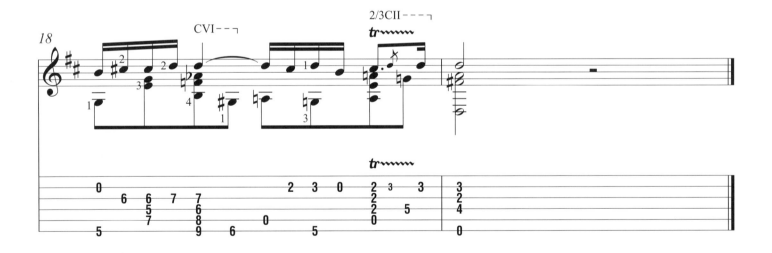

Prelude in C

Johann Sebastian Bach
Arranged by Bridget Mermikides

Drop D tuning:
(low to high) D-A-D-G-B-E

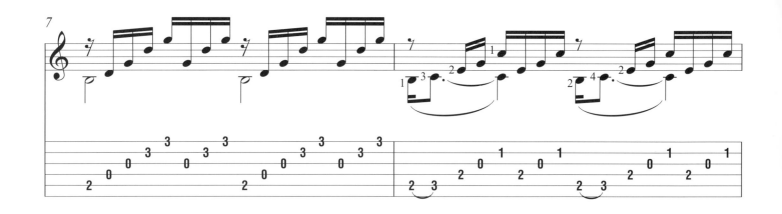

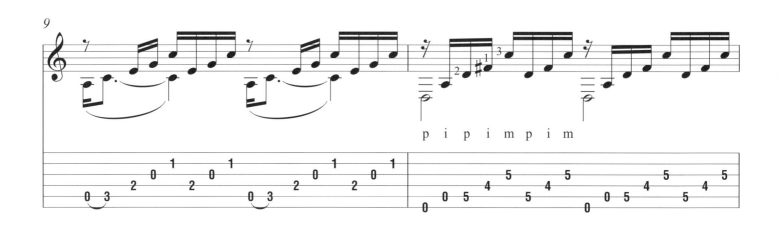

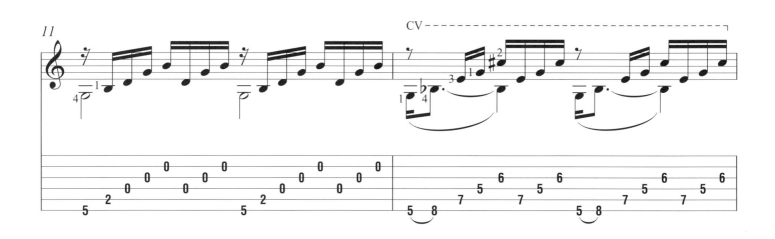

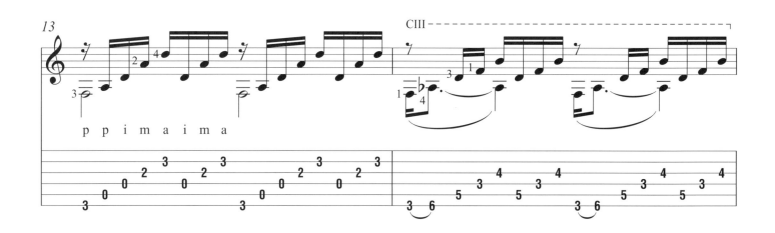

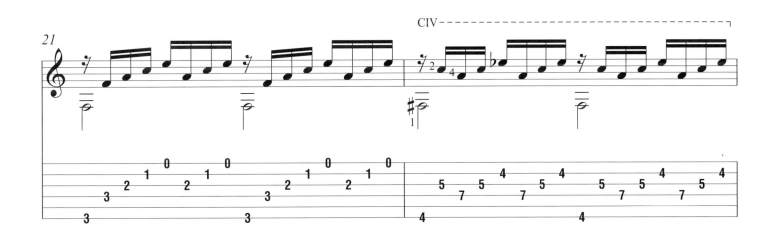

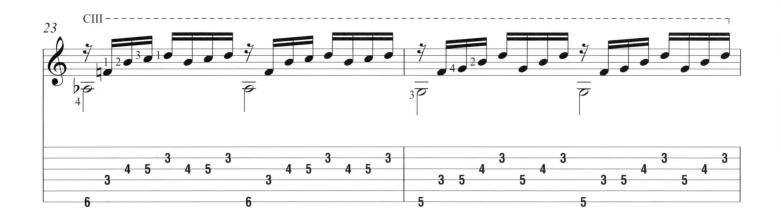
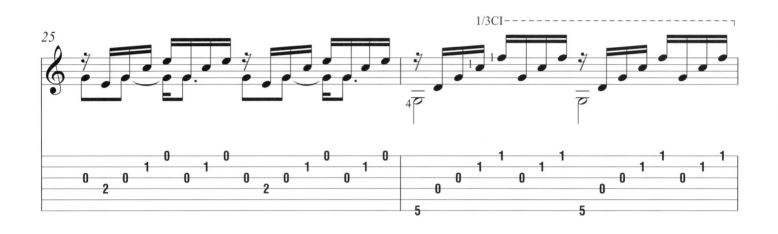

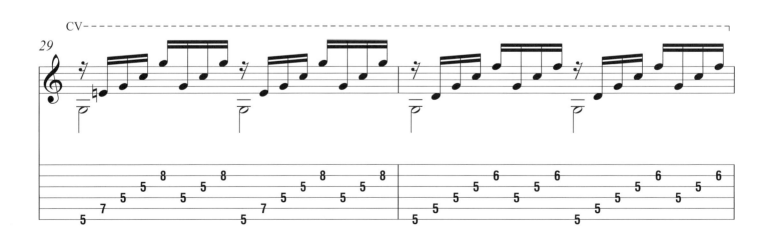

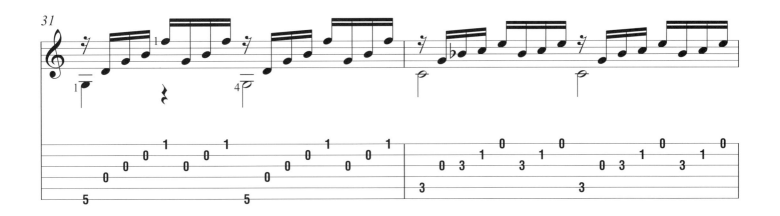

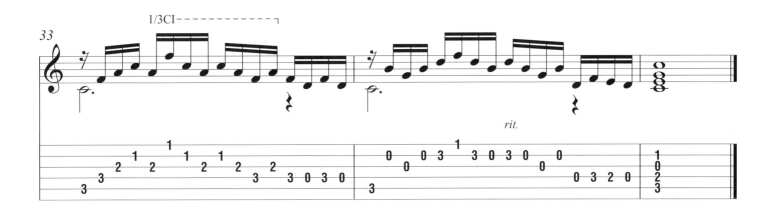

Prelude in D Minor, BWV 999

Johann Sebastian Bach
Arranged by Bridget Mermikides

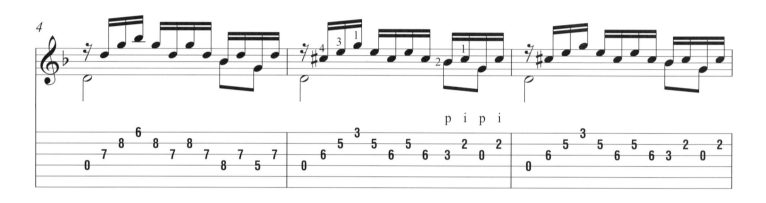

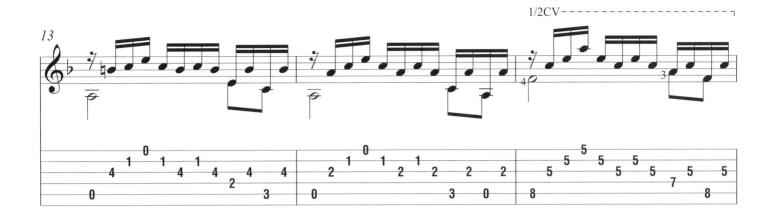

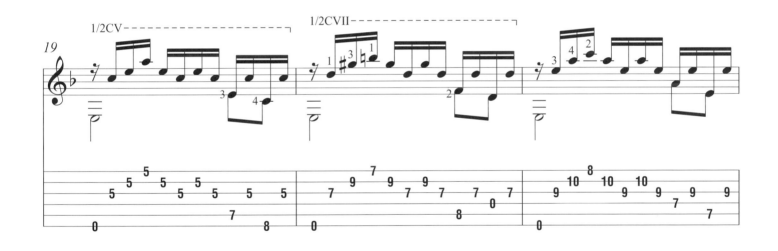

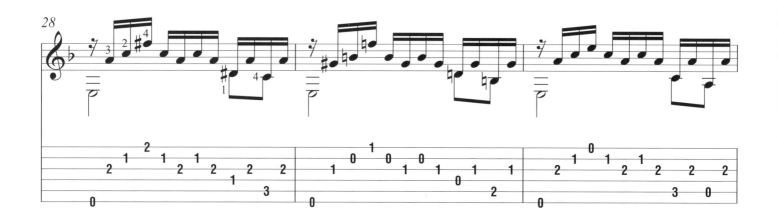

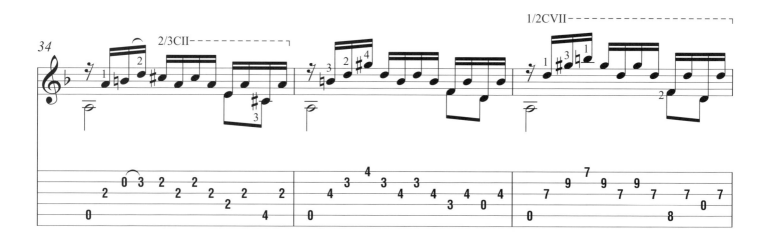

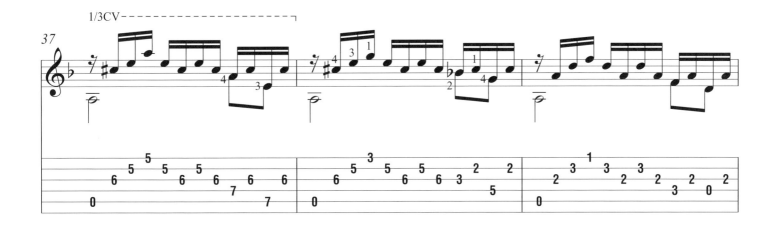

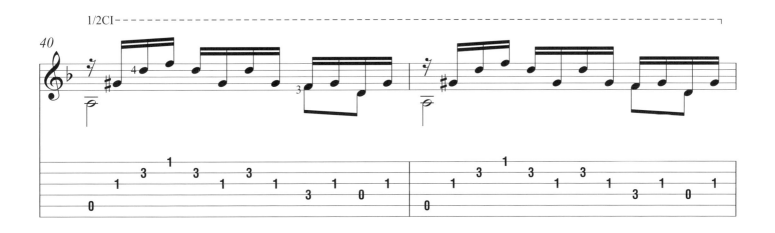

Minuet in G

Johann Sebastian Bach
Arranged by Bridget Mermikides

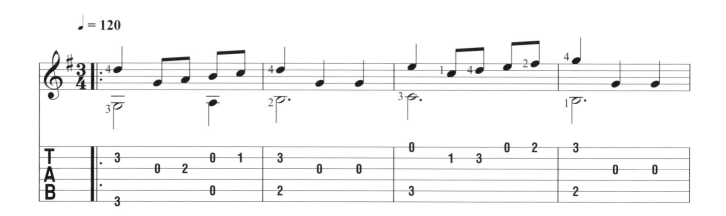

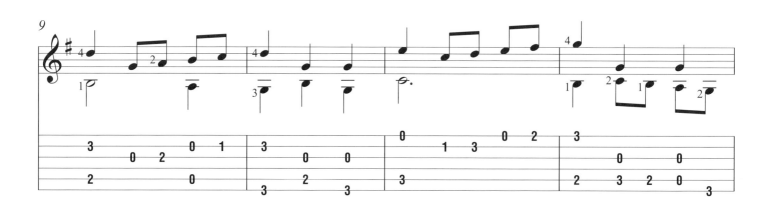

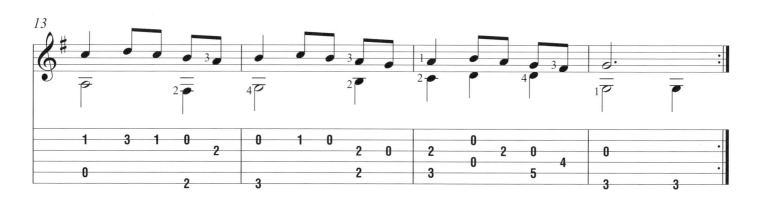

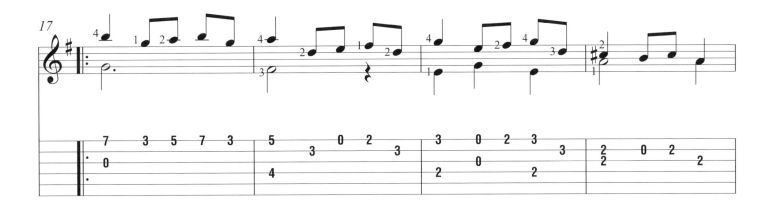

Ode to Joy

Ludwig van Beethoven
Arranged by Bridget Mermikides

Drop D tuning:
(low to high) D-A-D-G-B-E

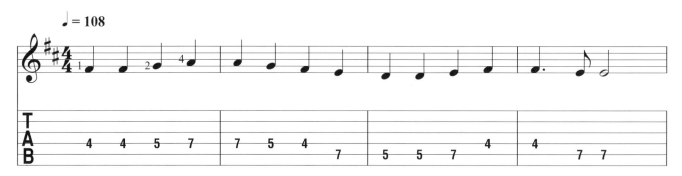

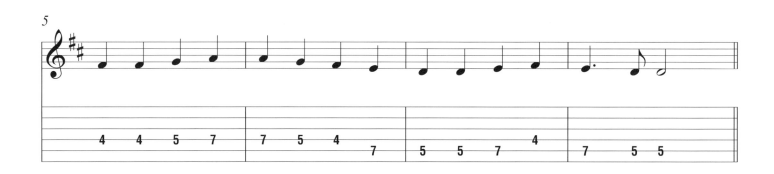

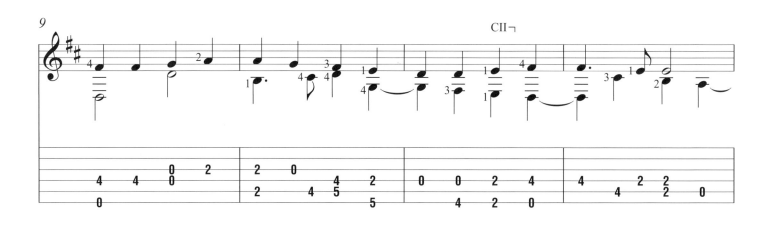

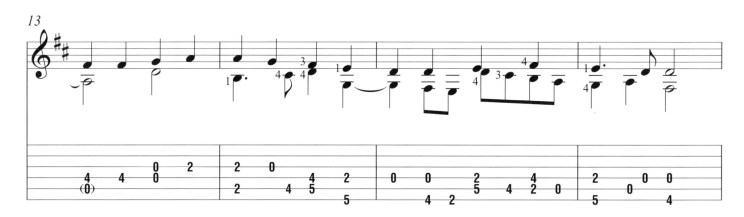

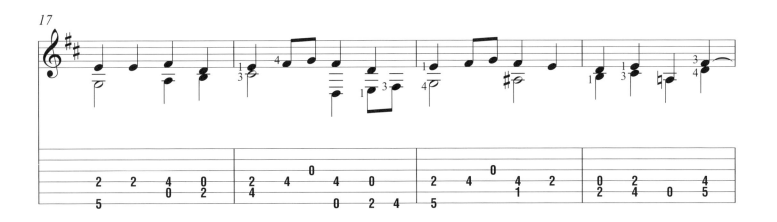

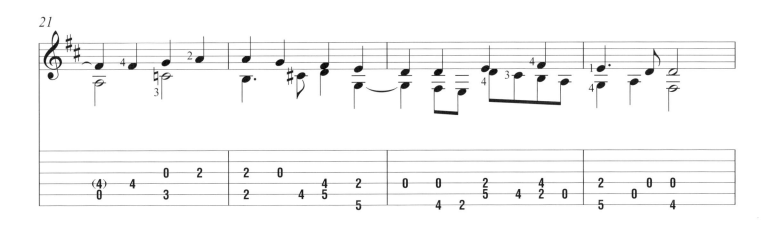

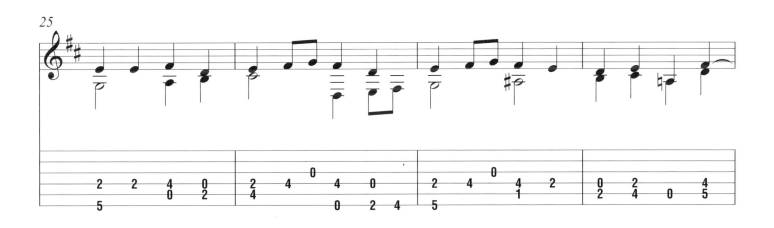

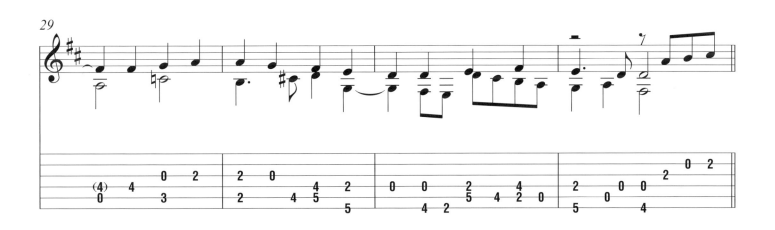

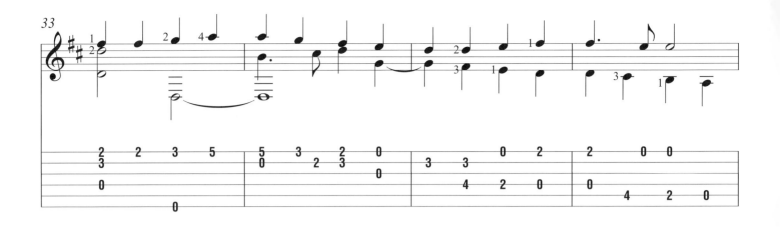

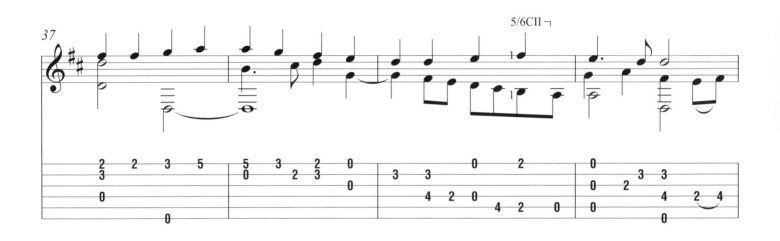

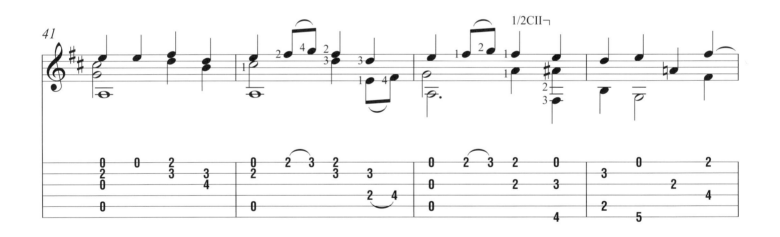

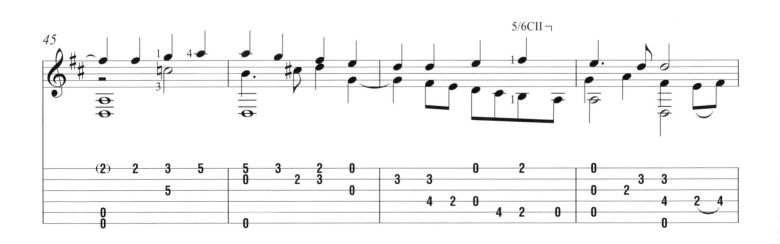

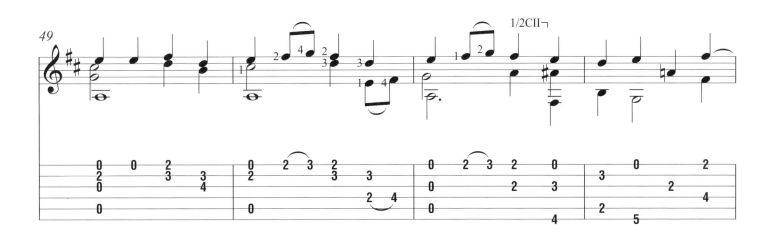

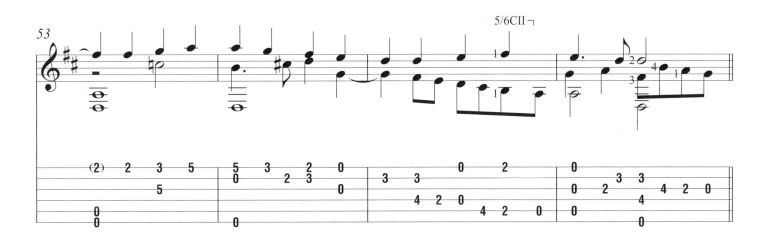

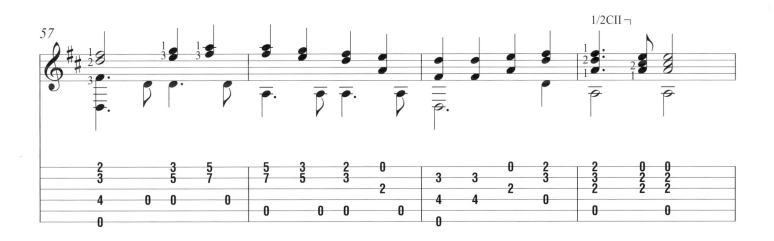

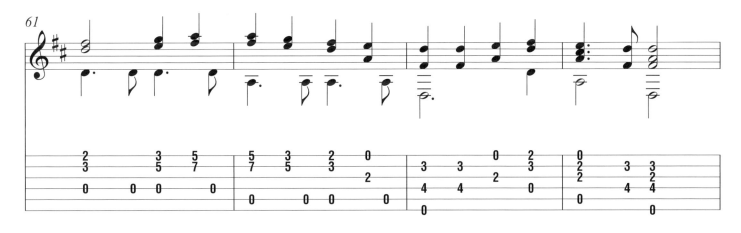

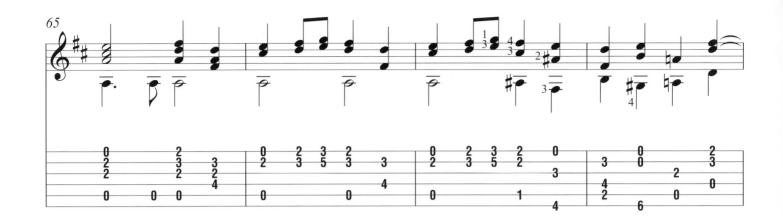

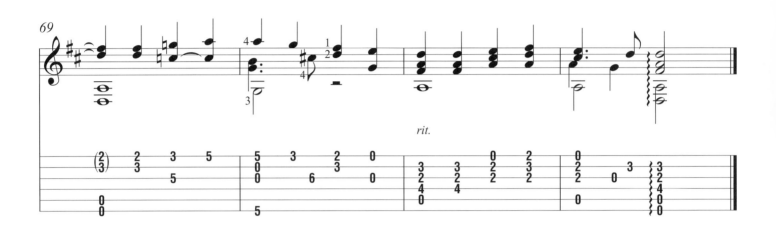

Minuet and Trio

Luigi Boccherini
Arranged by Bridget Mermikides

MINUETTO

♩ = ca. 72

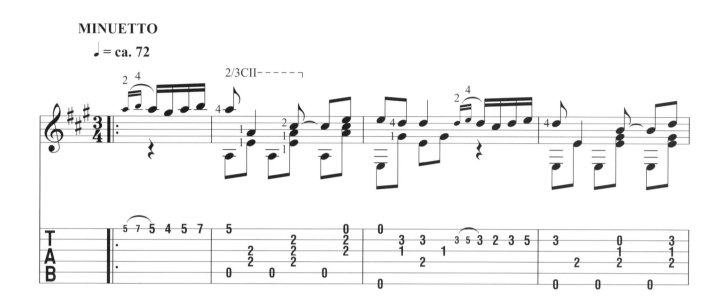

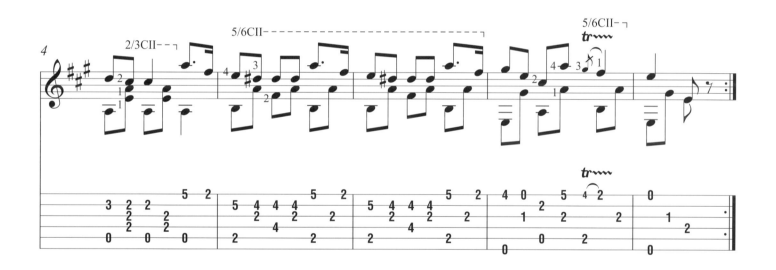

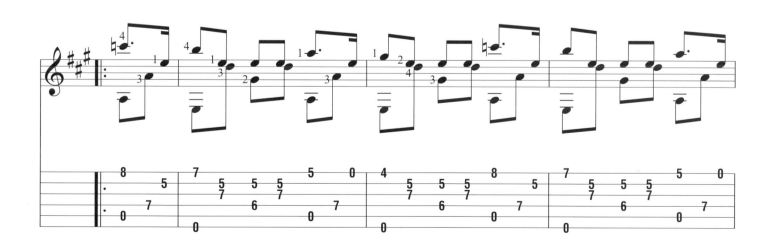

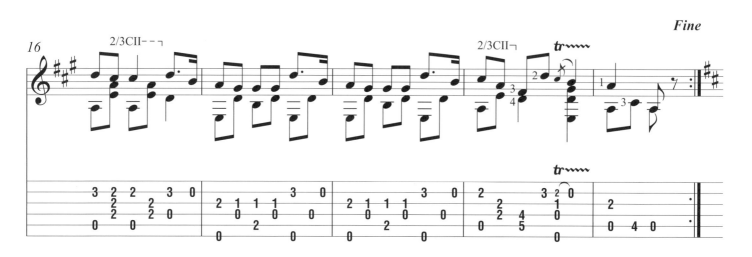

TRIO
♩ = ca. 92

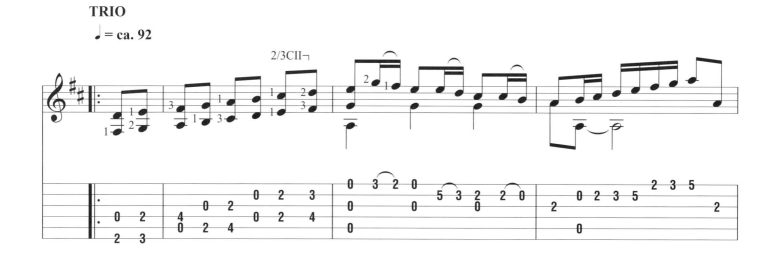

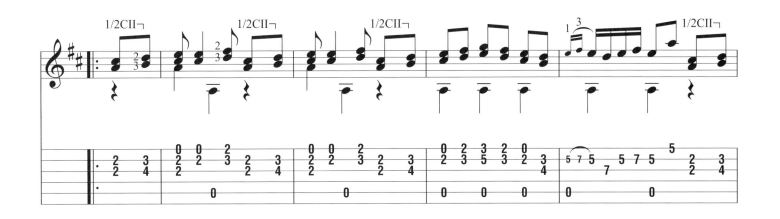

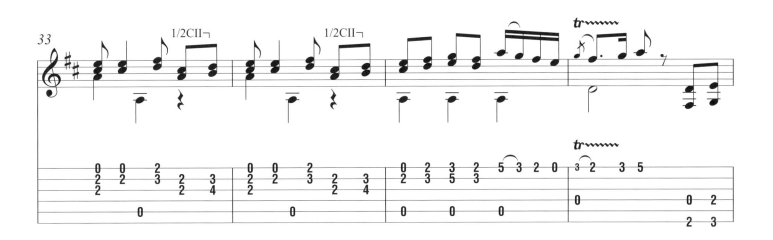

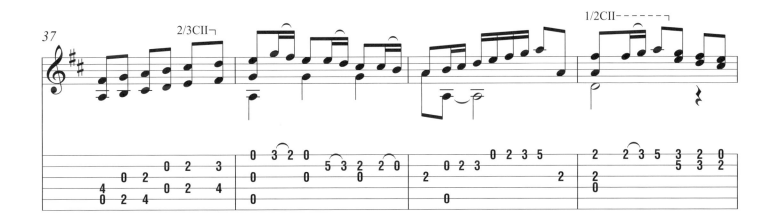

2nd time, D.C. al Fine
(no repeats)

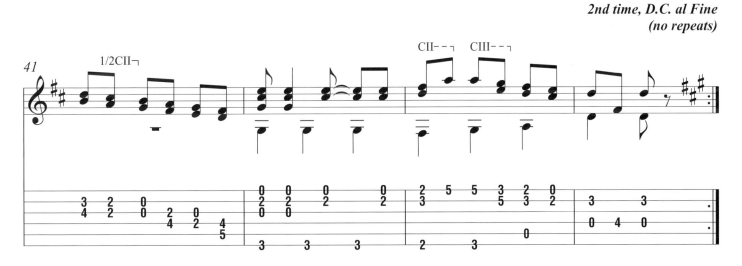

Habanera

Georges Bizet

Arranged by Bridget Mermikides

Drop D tuning:
(low to high) D-A-D-G-B-E

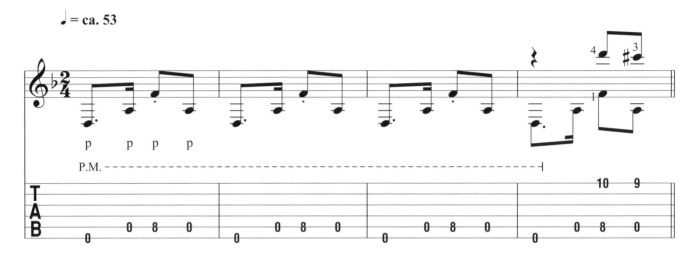

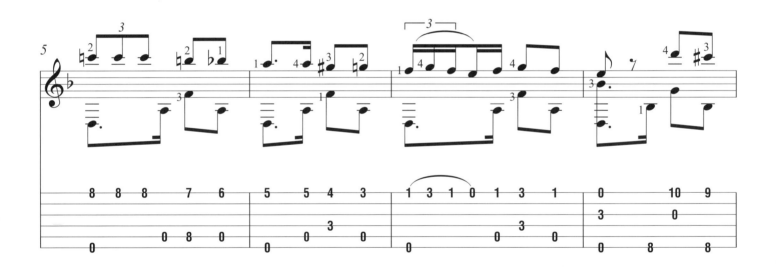

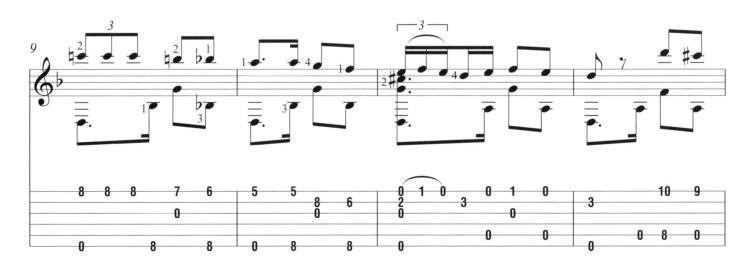

O Solé Mio

Eduardo di Capua
Arranged by Bridget Mermikides

Drop D tuning:
(low to high) D-A-D-G-B-E

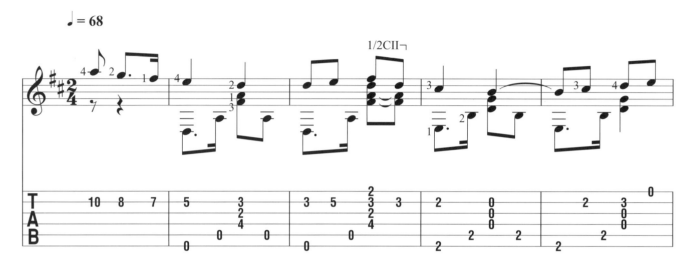

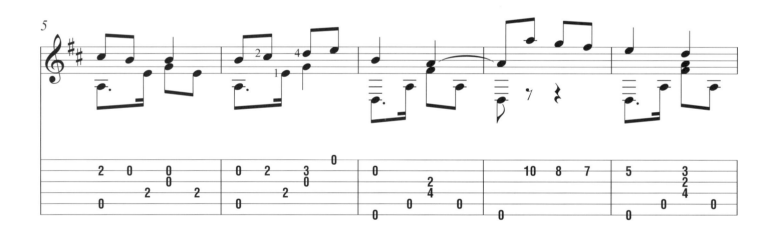

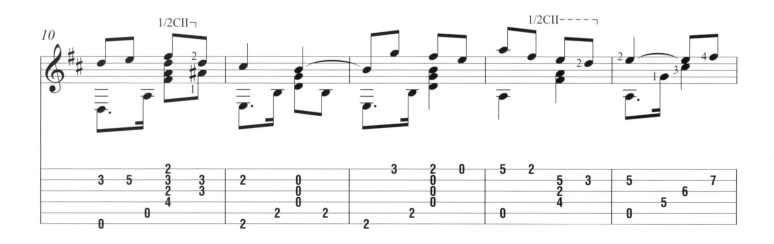

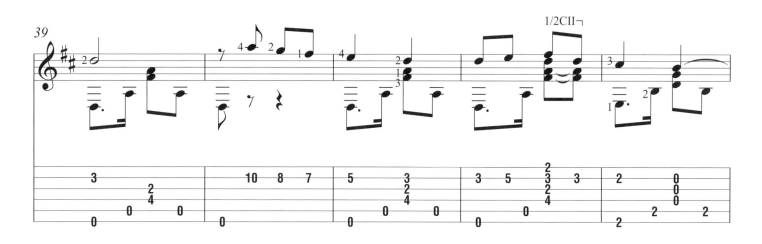
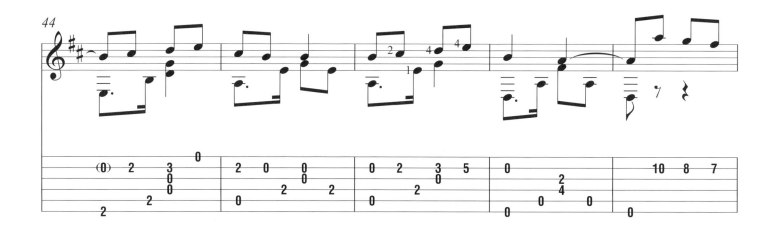
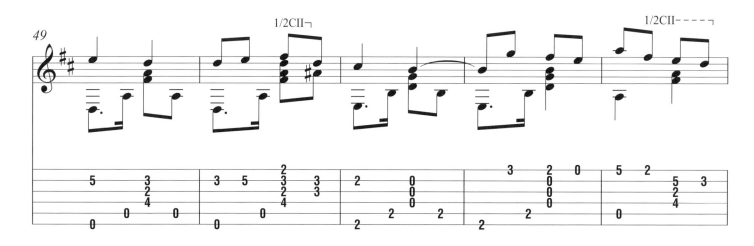

Nimrod

Edward Elgar
Arranged by Bridget Mermikides

Drop D tuning:
(low to high) D-A-D-G-B-E

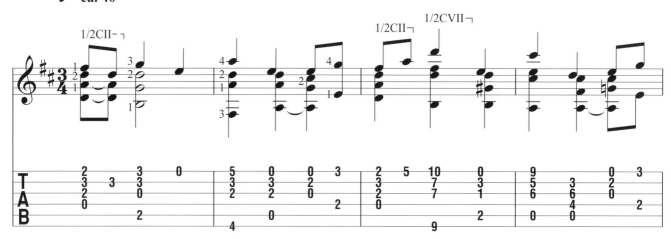

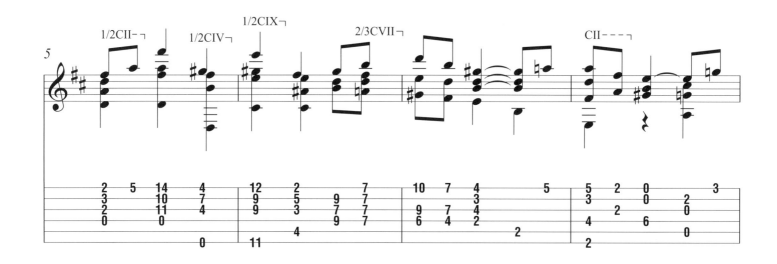

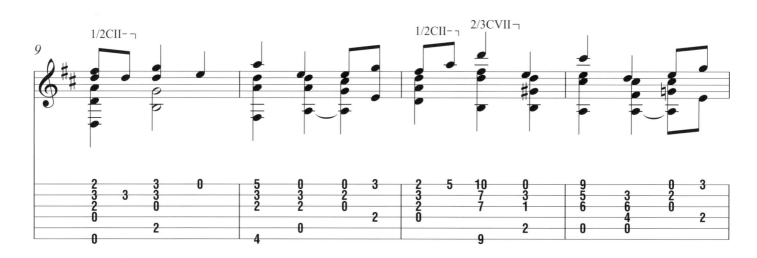

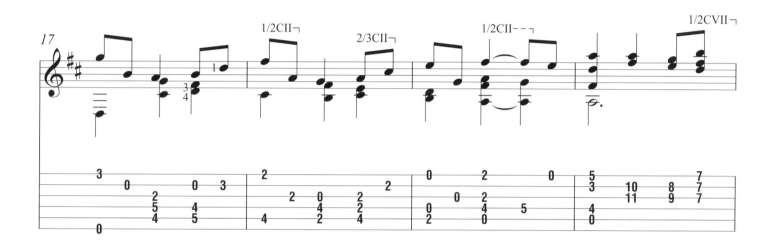

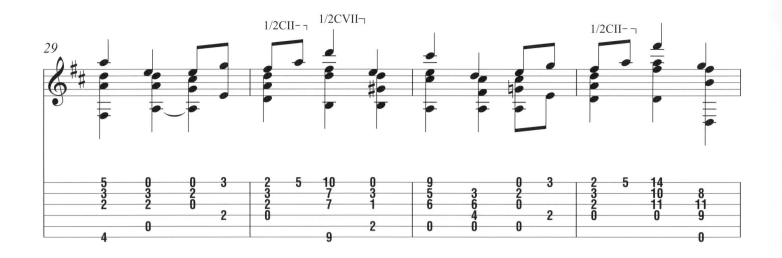

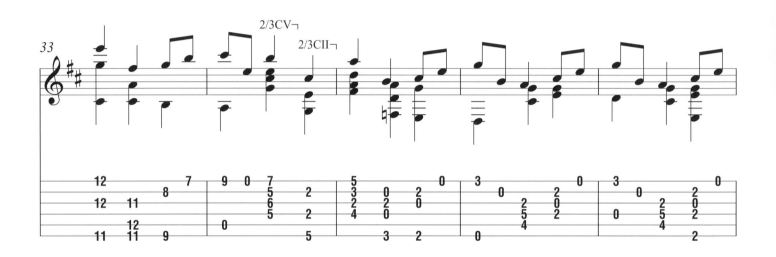

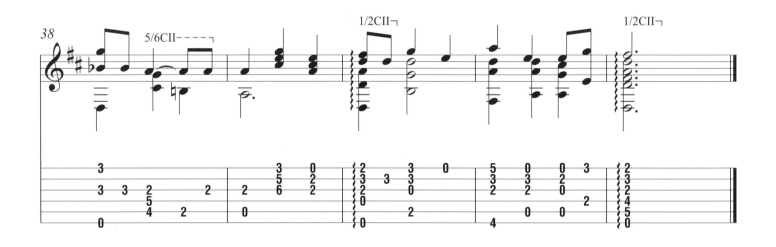

Solveig's Song

Edvard Grieg
Arranged by Bridget Mermikides

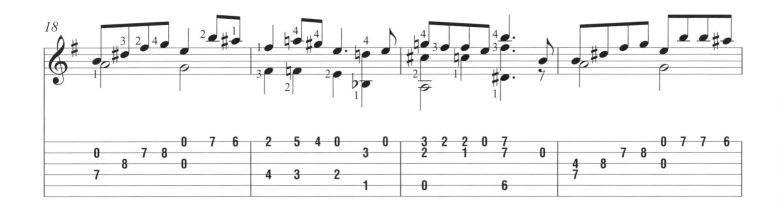

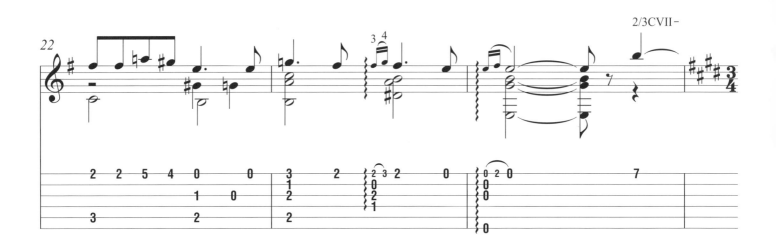

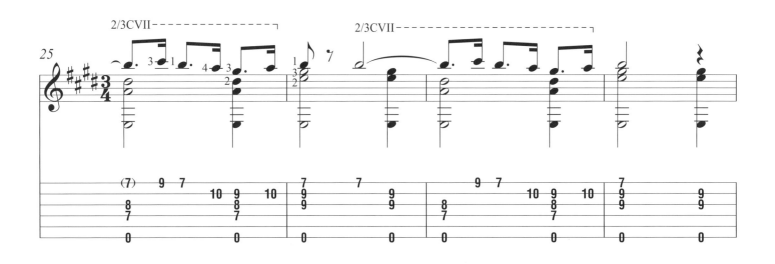

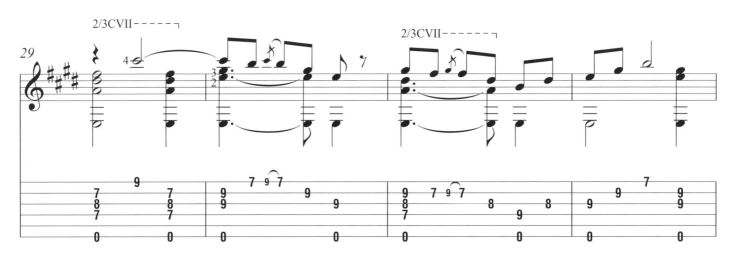

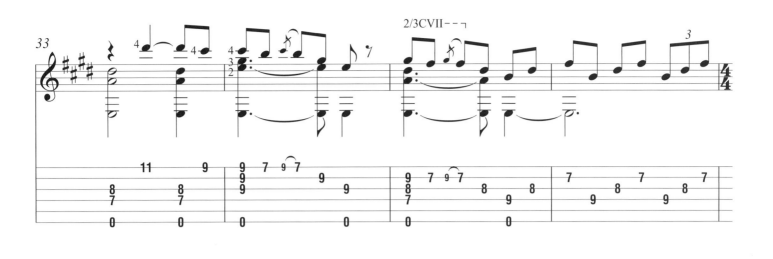

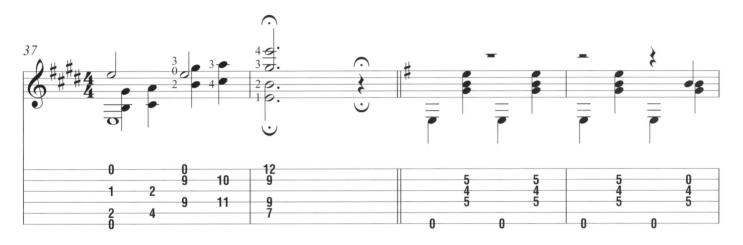

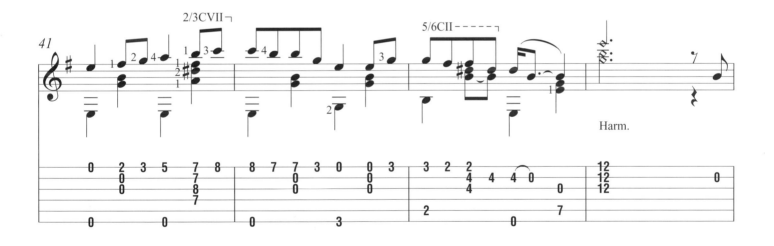

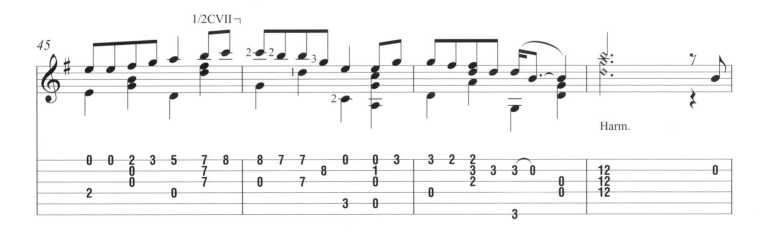

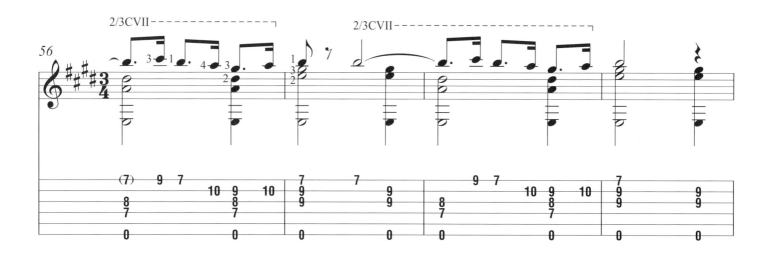

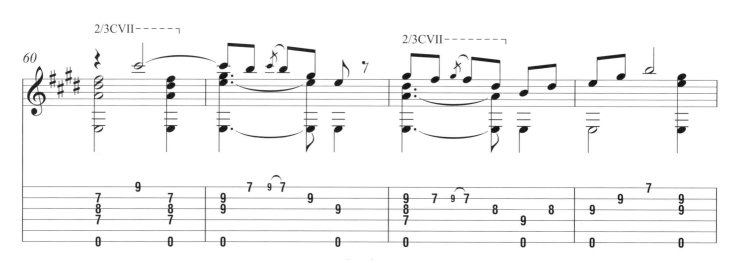

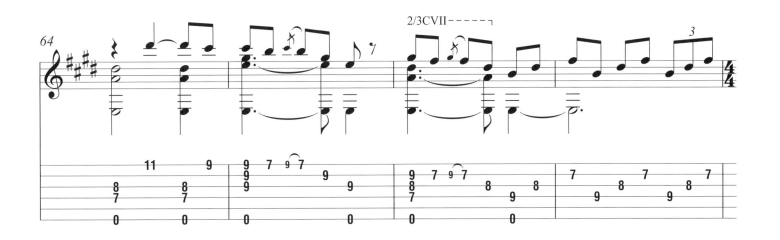

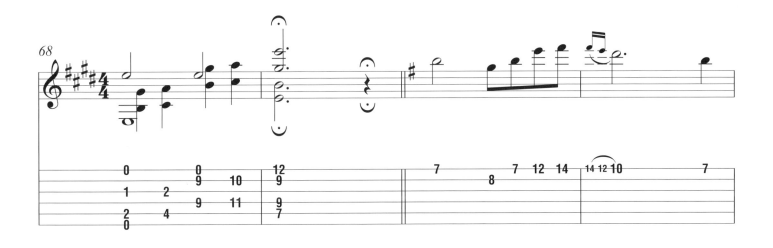

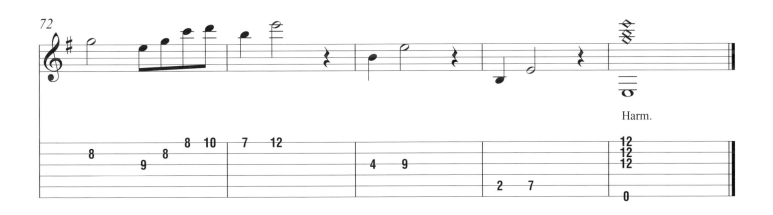

New World Symphony (Theme)

Antonín Dvořák
Arranged by Bridget Mermikides

Tuning:
(low to high) C-G-C-G-C-E

♩ = ca. 37

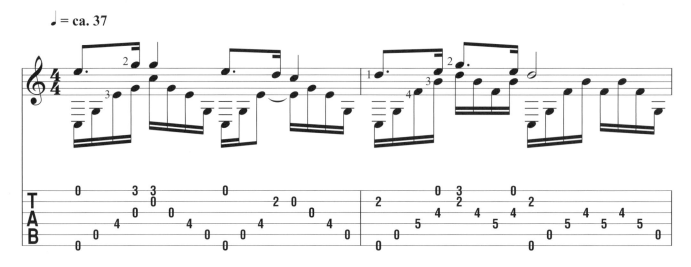

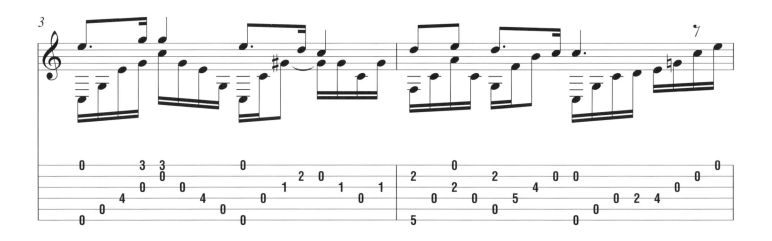

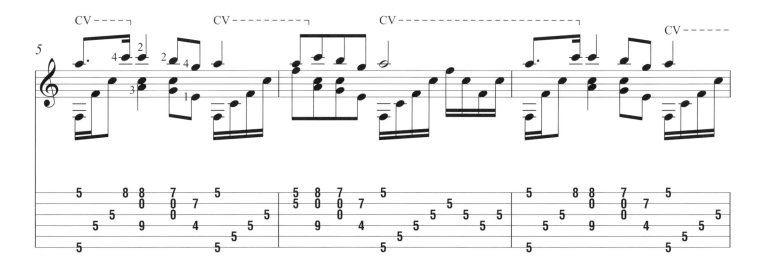

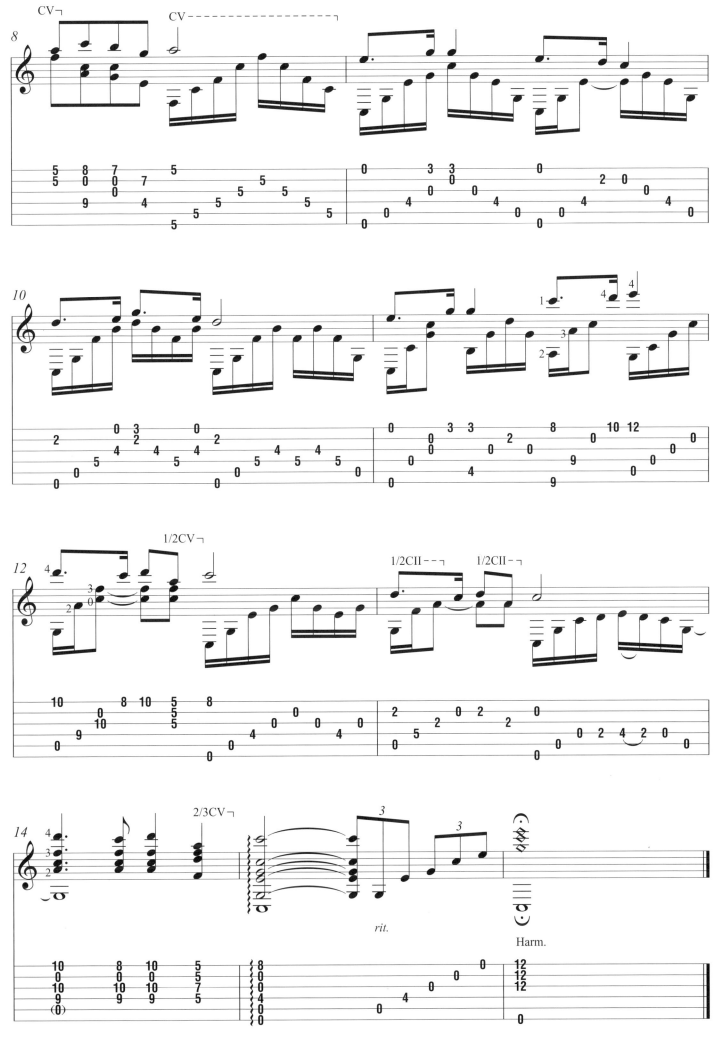

Eine Kleine Nachtmusik

Wolfgang Amadeus Mozart
Arranged by Bridget Mermikides

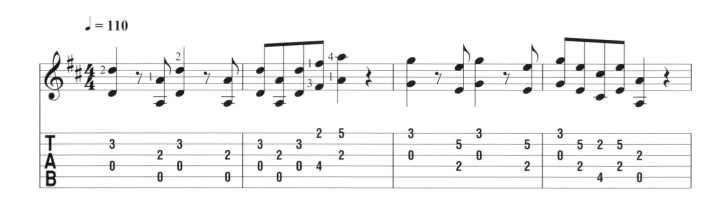

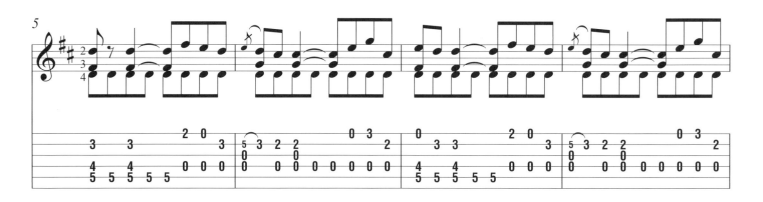

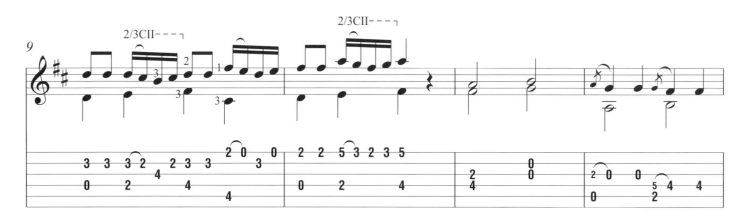

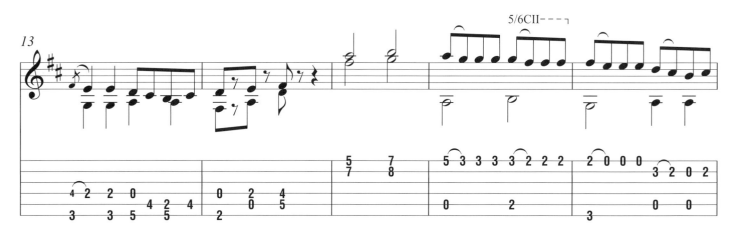

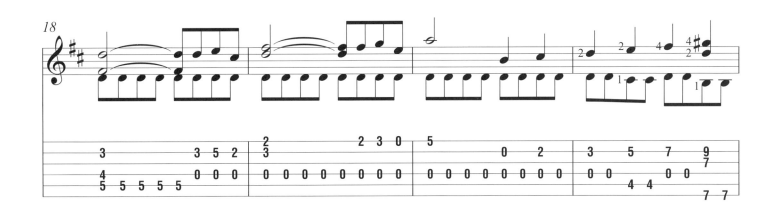

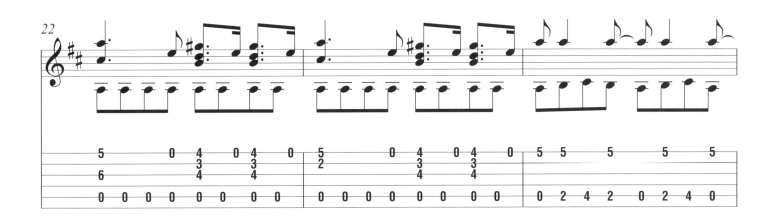

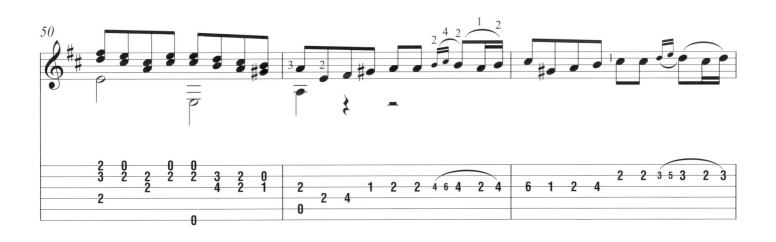

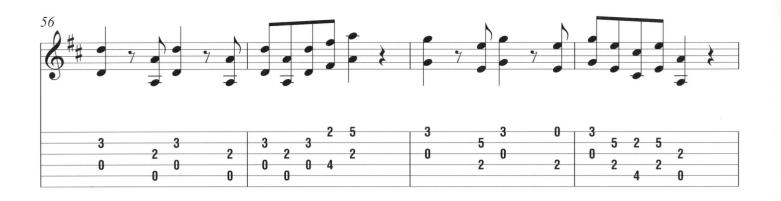

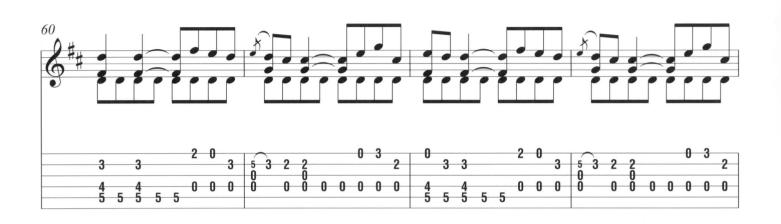

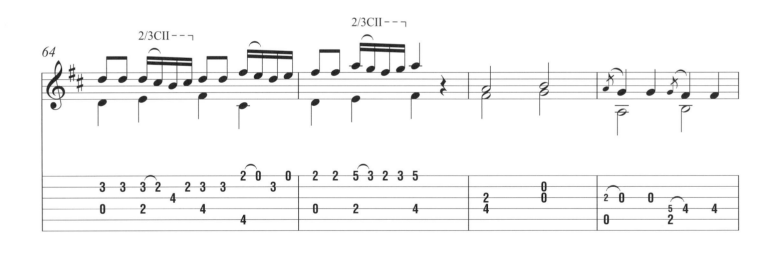

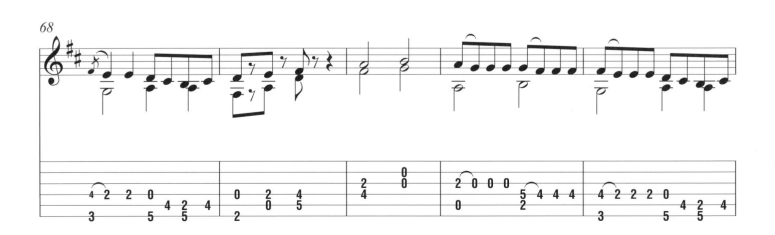

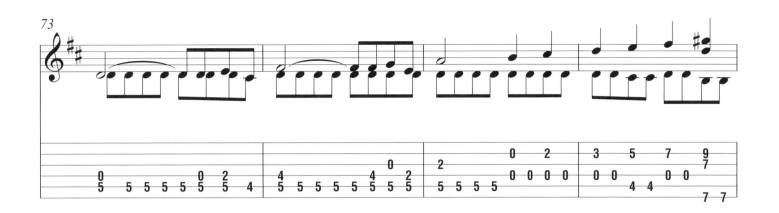

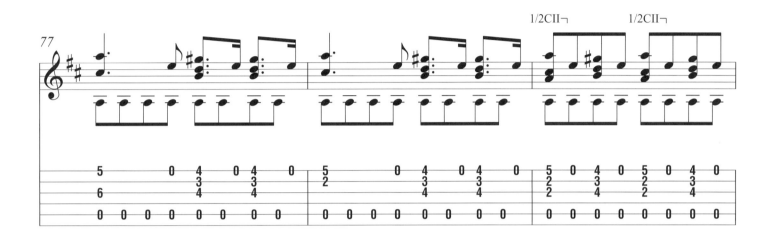

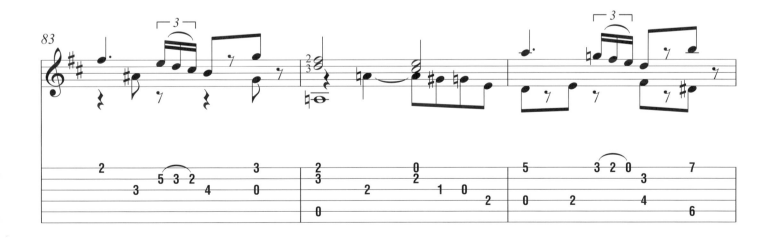

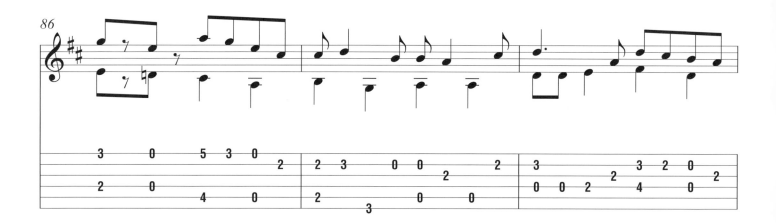

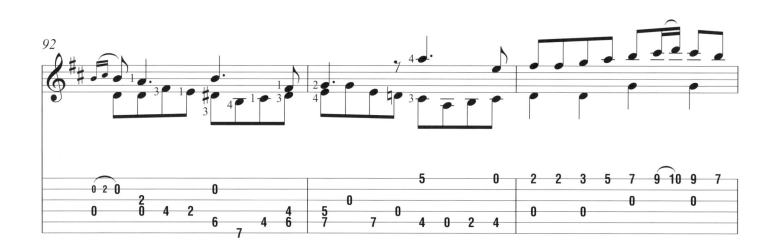

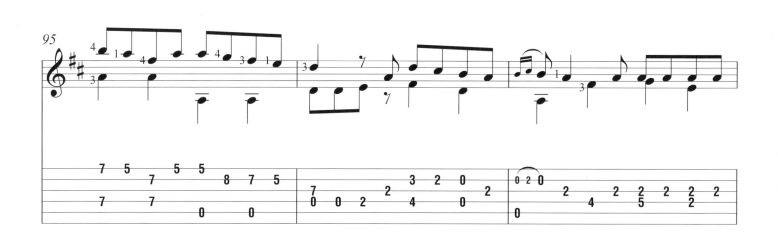

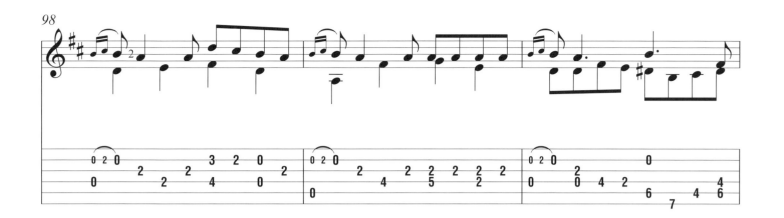

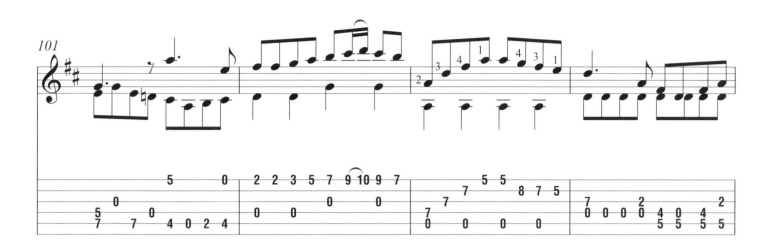

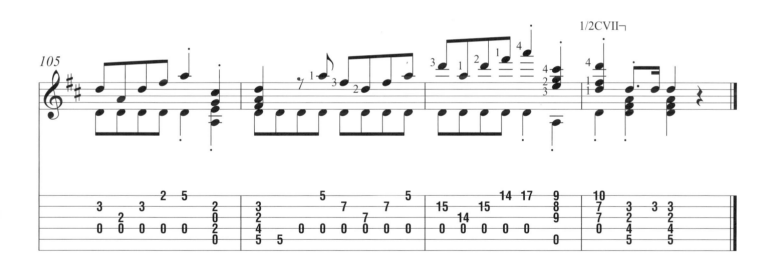

Symphony No. 40 (abridged)

Wolfgang Amadeus Mozart
Arranged by Bridget Mermikides

Drop D tuning:
(low to high) D-A-D-G-B-E

♩ = ca. 148

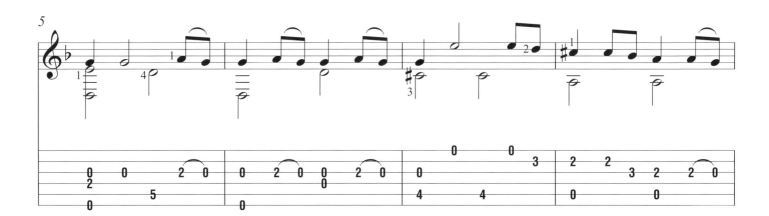

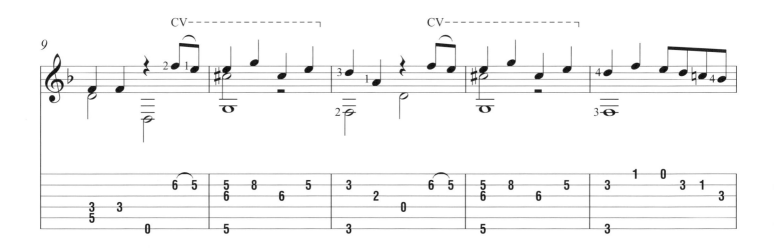

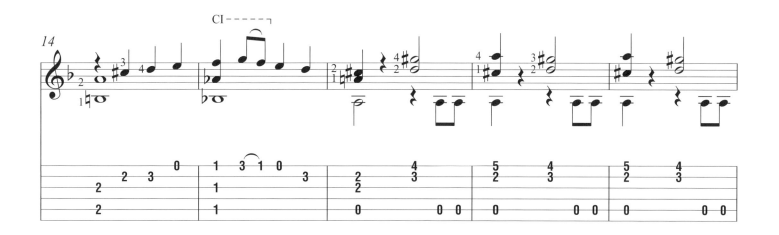

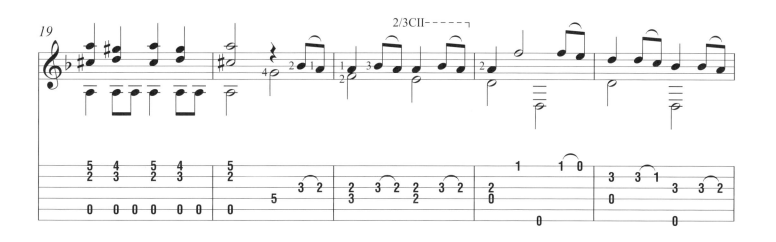

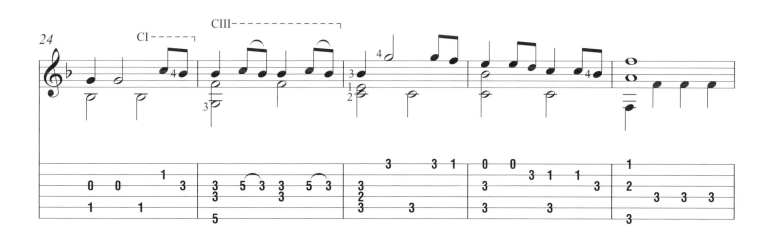

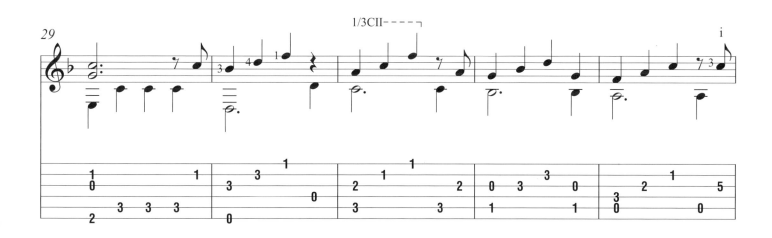

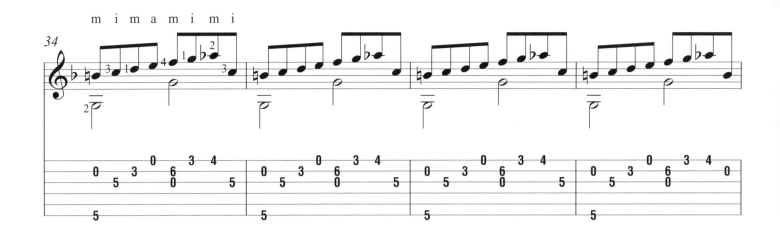

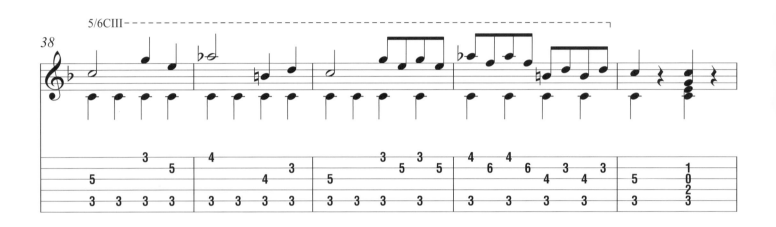

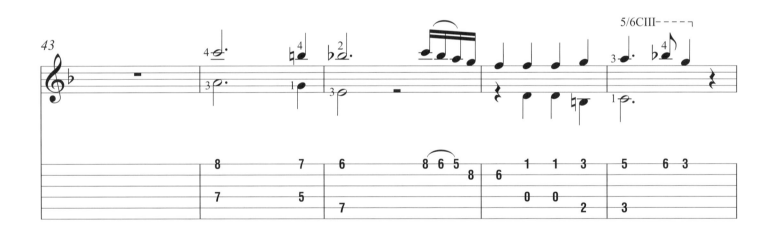

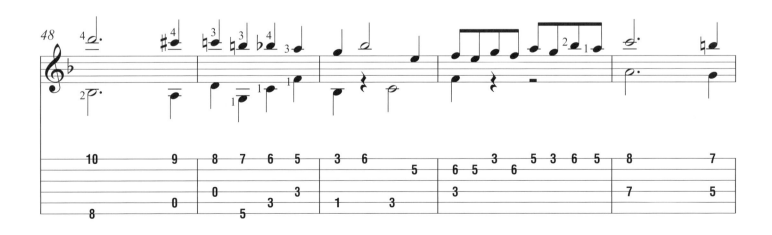

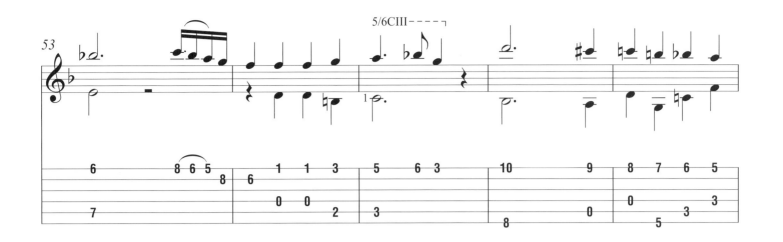

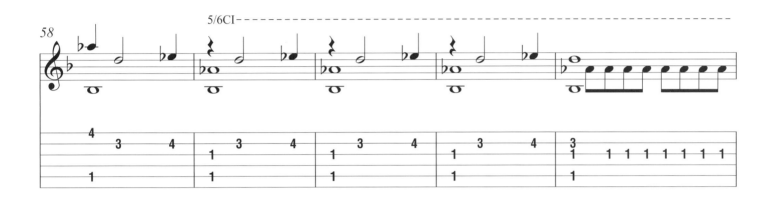

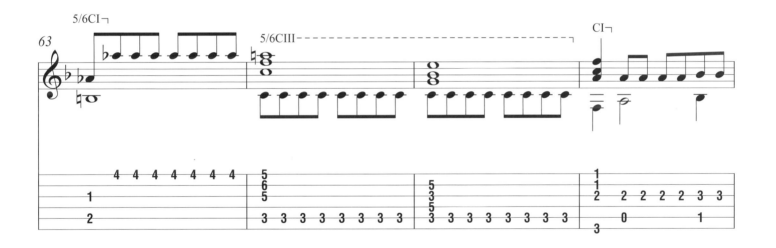

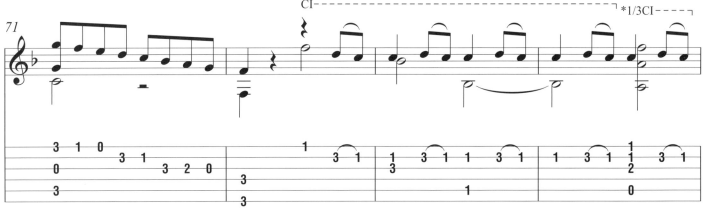

*w/ base segment of finger

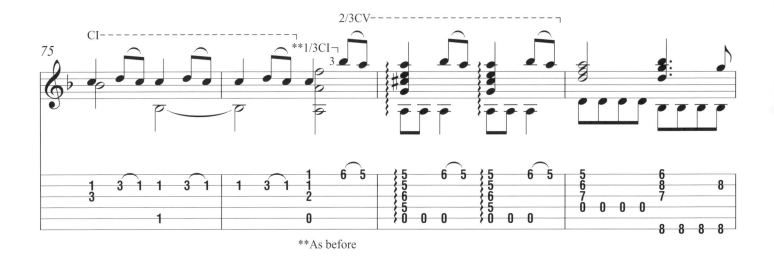

**As before

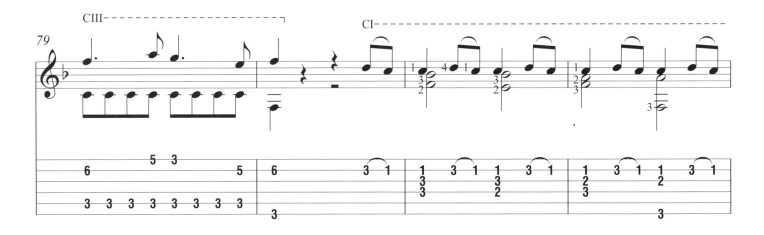

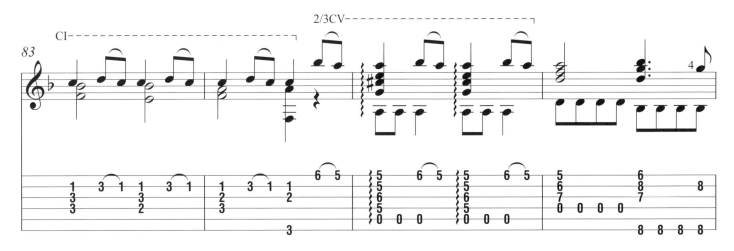

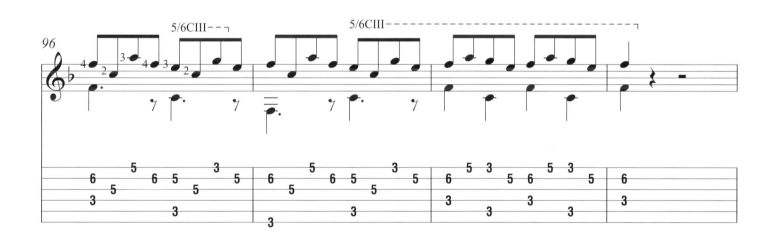

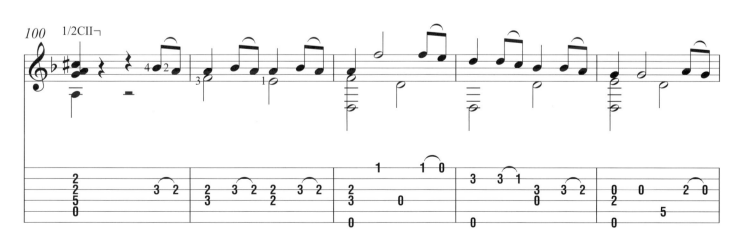

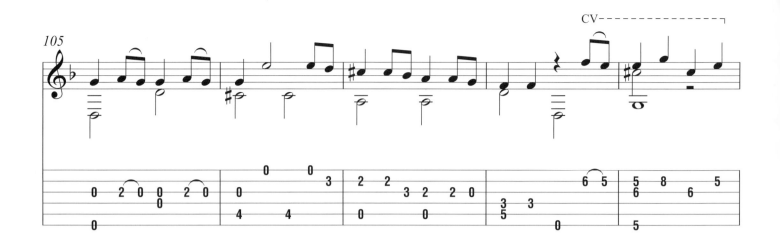

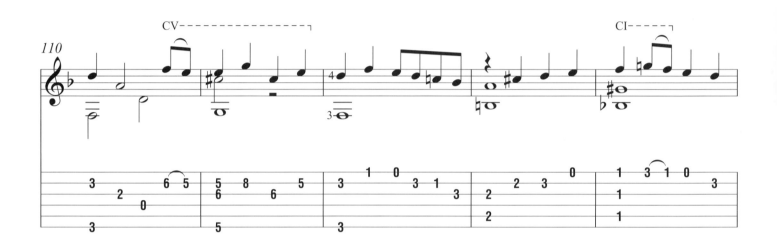

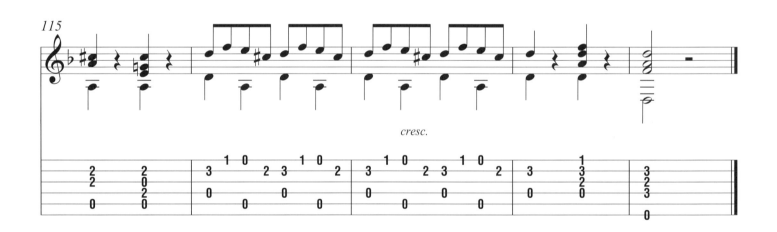

O Mio Babbino Caro

Giacomo Puccini
Arranged by Bridget Mermikides

Drop D tuning:
(low to high) D-A-D-G-B-E

*2nd-4th strings only.

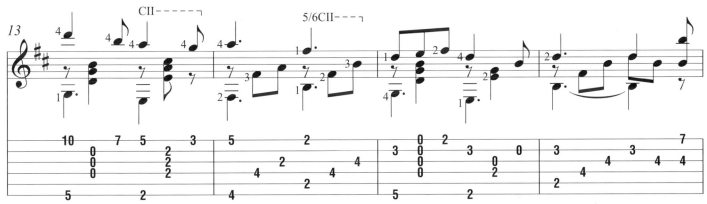

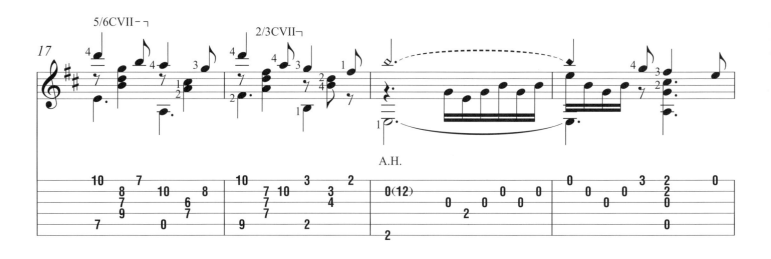

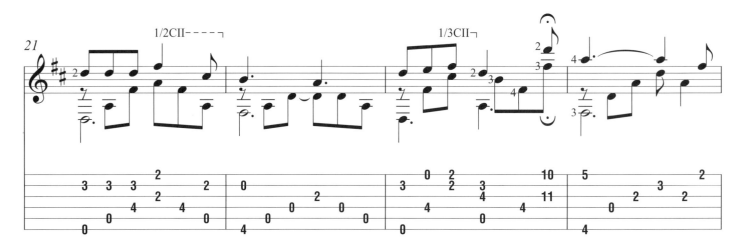

*As before

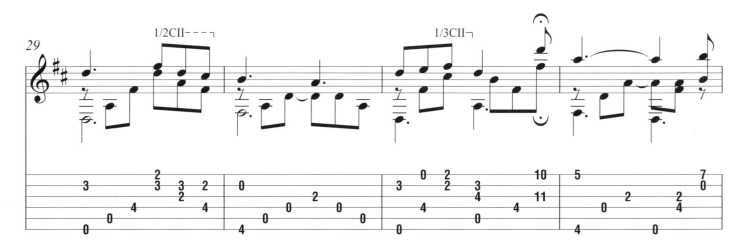

Pictures at an Exhibition
Promenade Theme

Modest Mussorgsky
Arranged by Bridget Mermikides

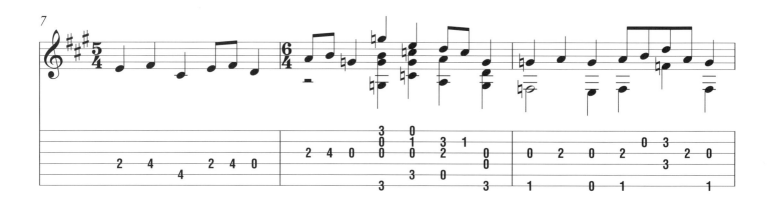

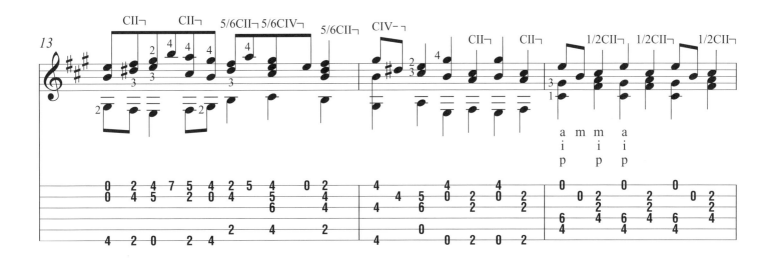

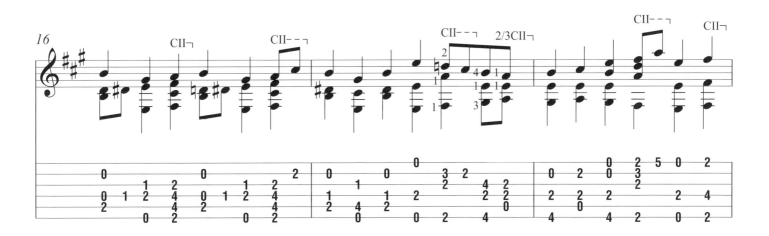

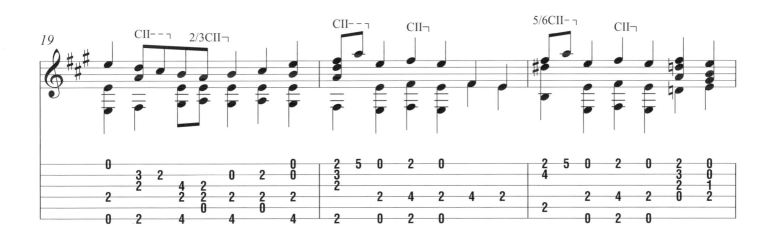

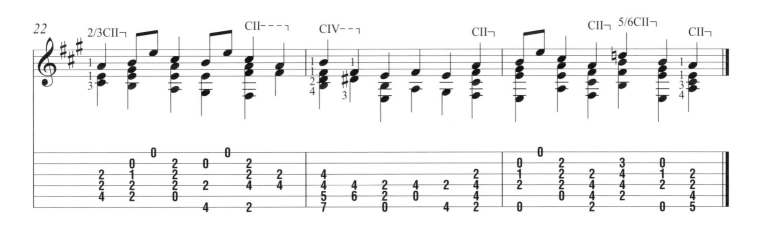

Jerusalem

Hubert Parry
Arranged by Bridget Mermikides

Drop D tuning:
(low to high) D-A-D-G-B-E

♩ = 53

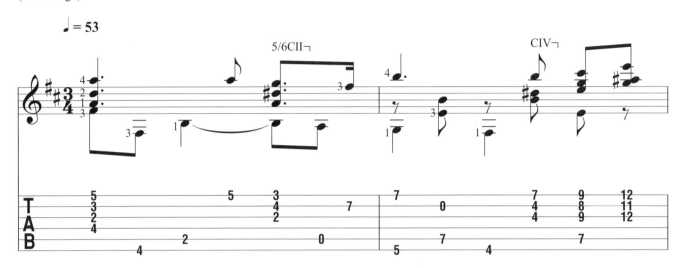

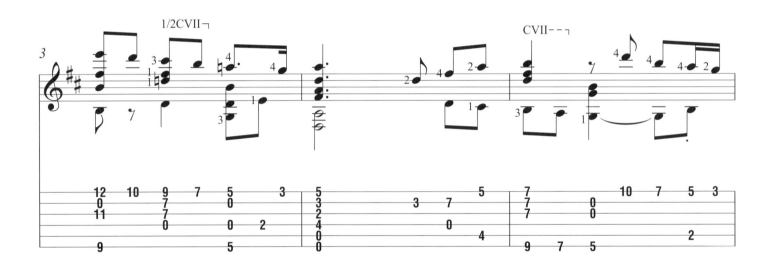

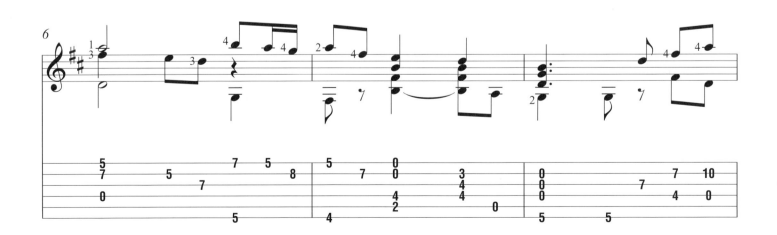

*2nd-4th strings only.

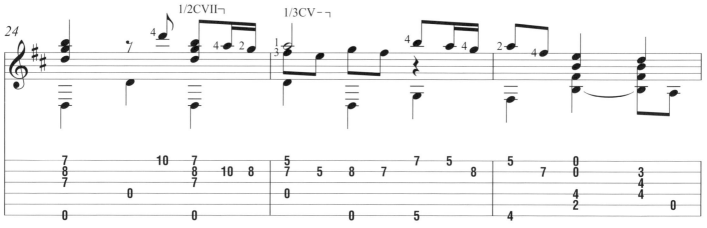

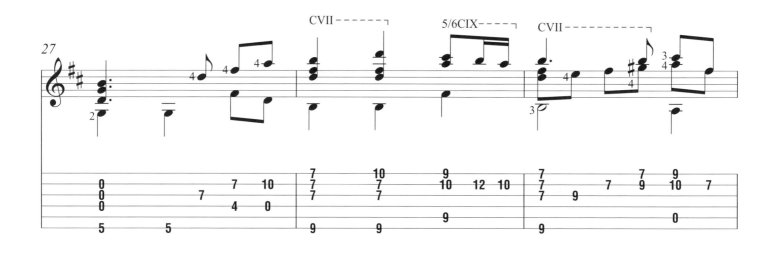

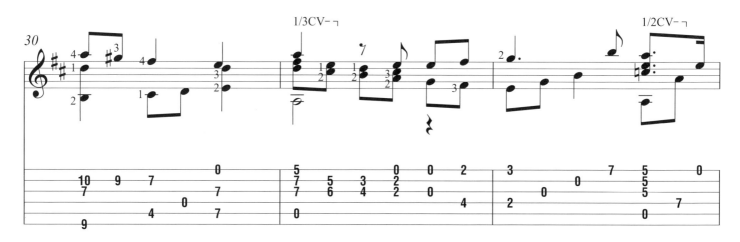

The Aquarium

Camille Saint-Saëns
Arranged by Bridget Mermikides

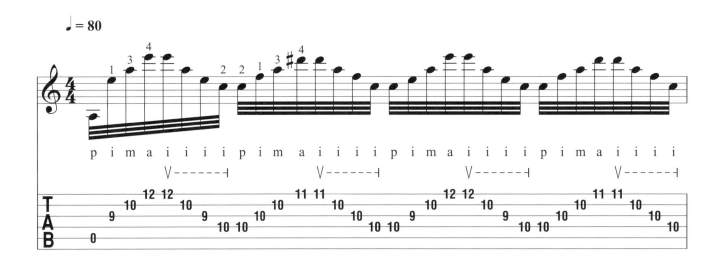

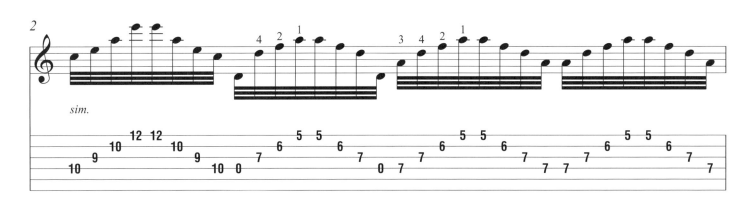

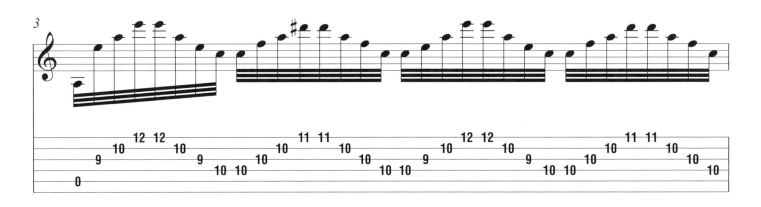

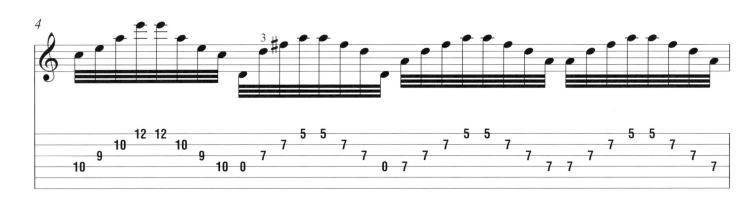

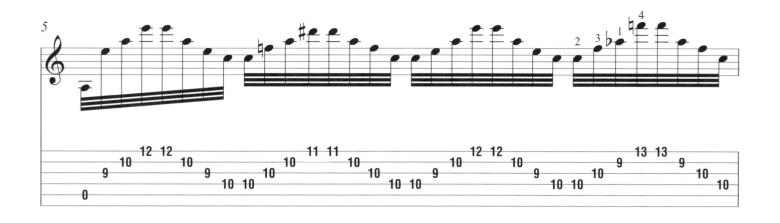

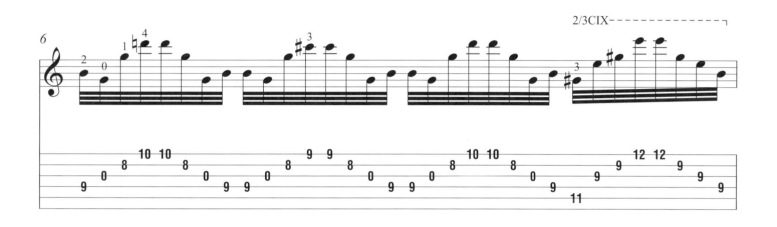

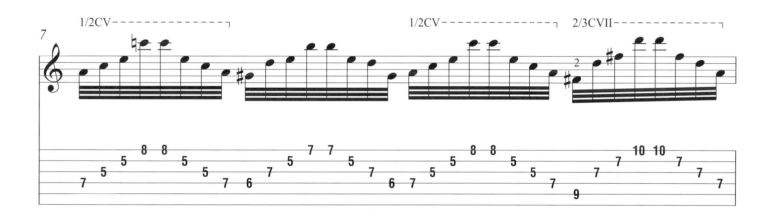

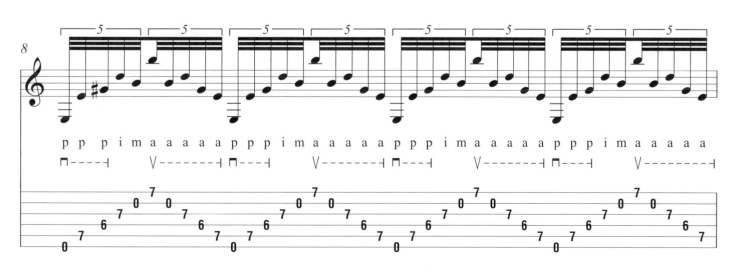

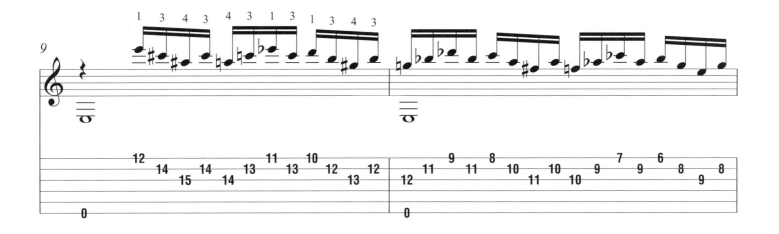

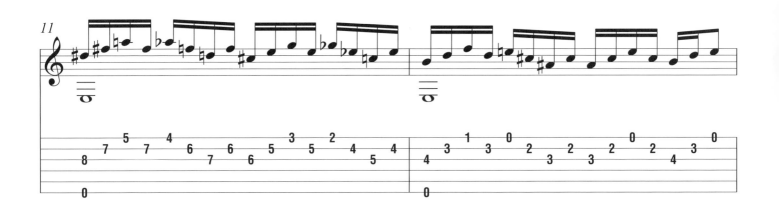

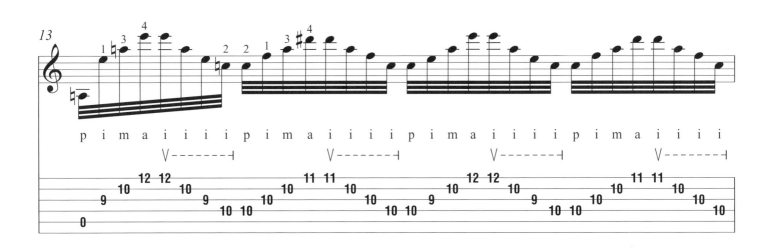

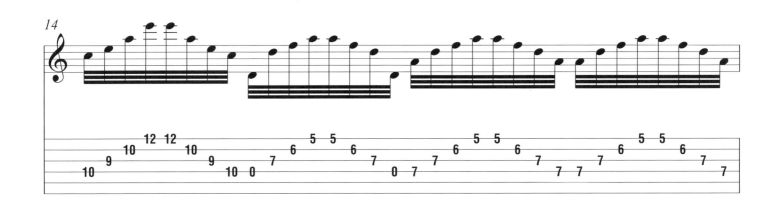

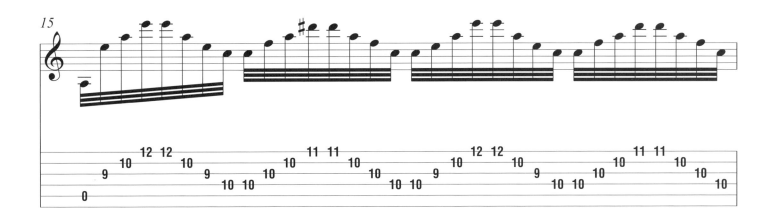

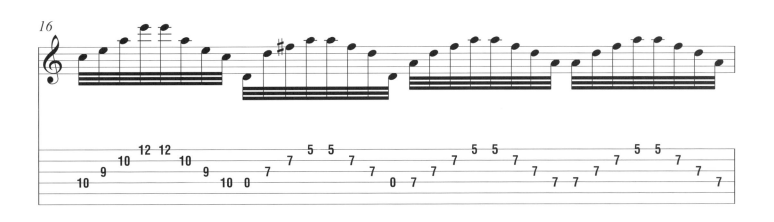

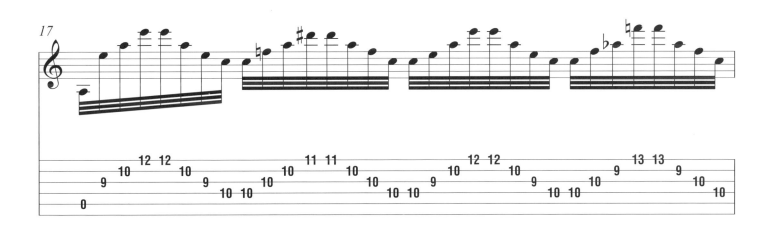

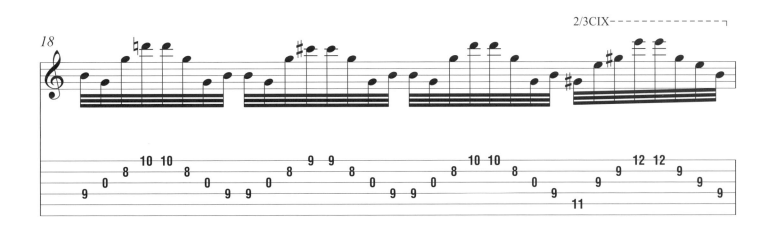

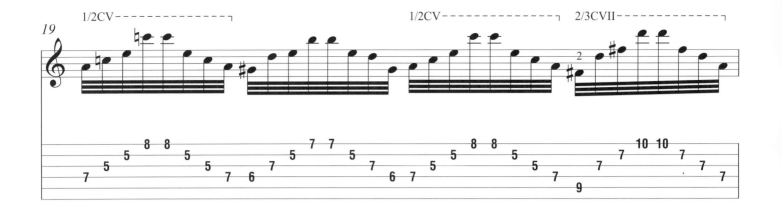

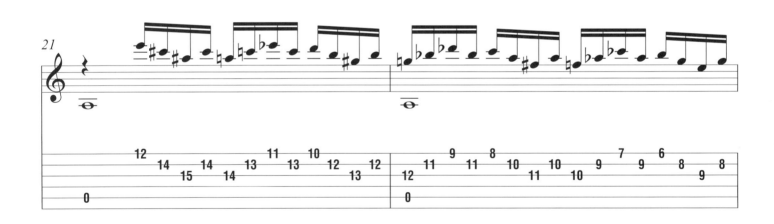

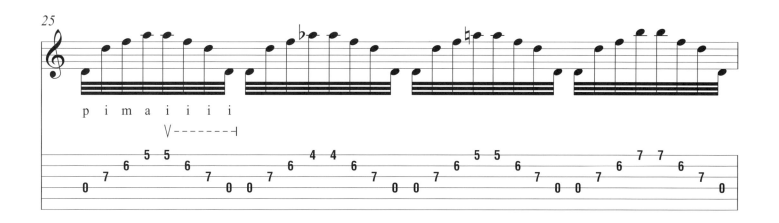

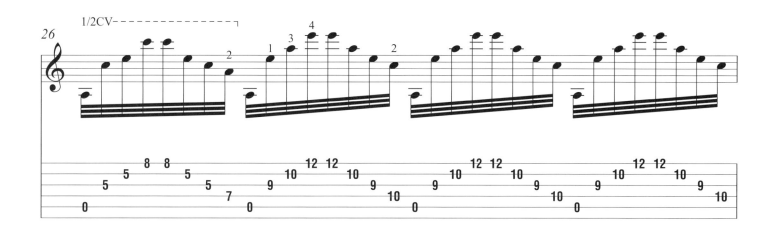

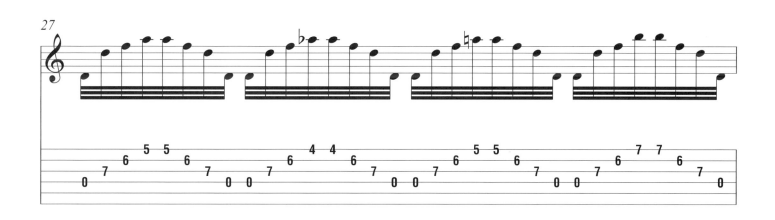

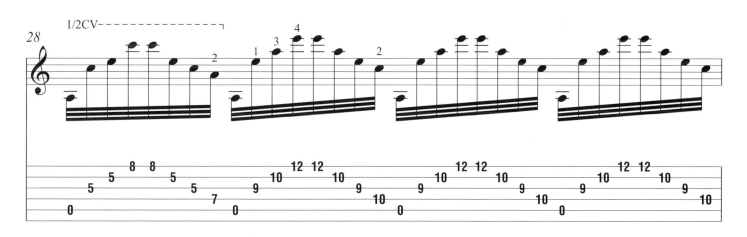

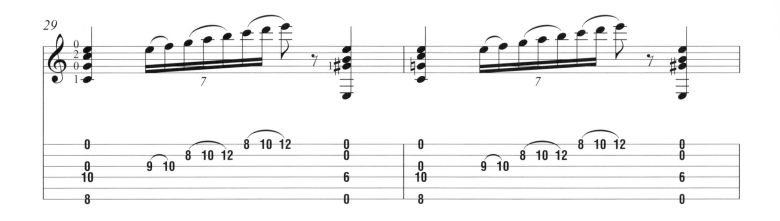

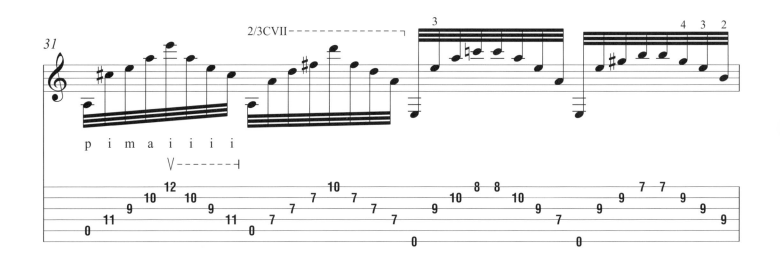

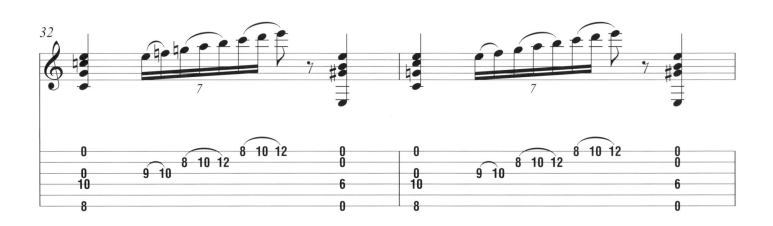

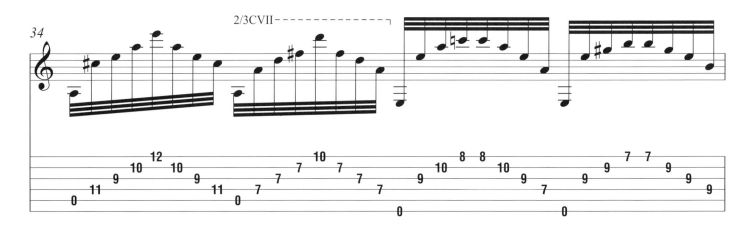

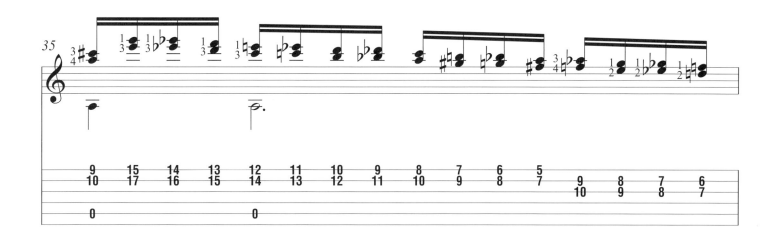

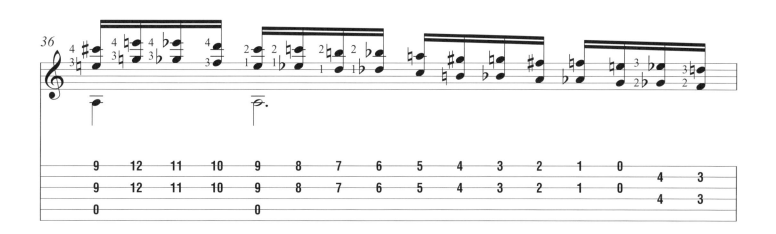

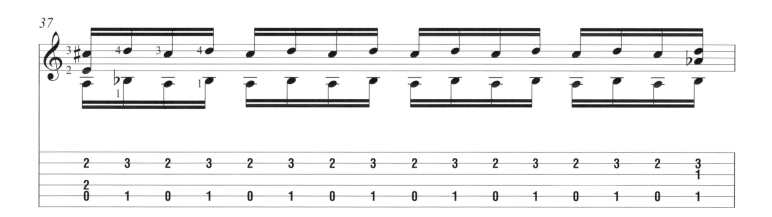

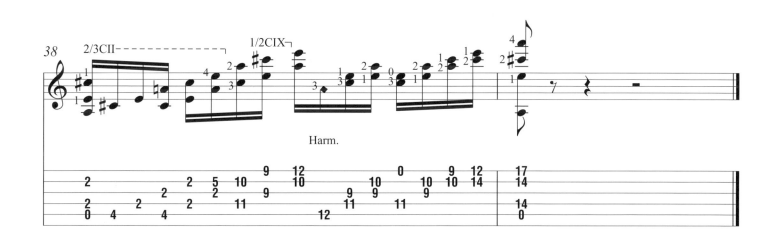

Gymnopédie No. 2

Erik Satie
Arranged by Bridget Mermikides

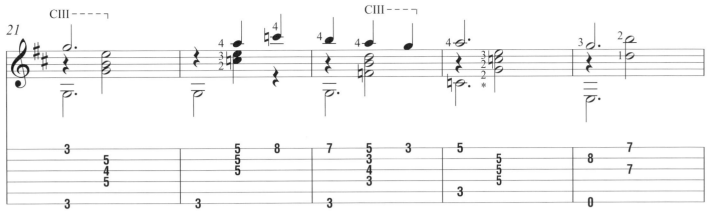

*Barre 3rd & 4th strings with 2nd finger.

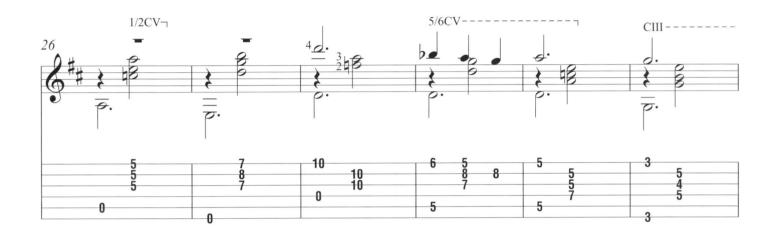

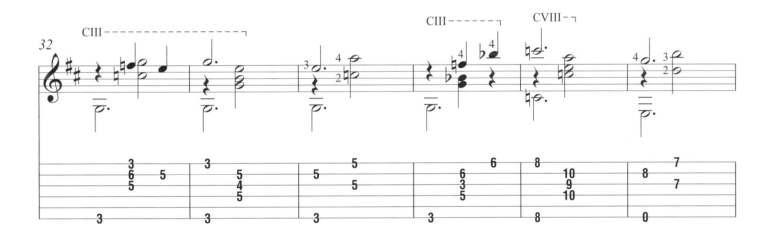

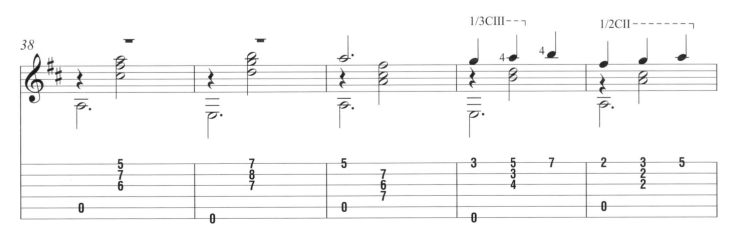

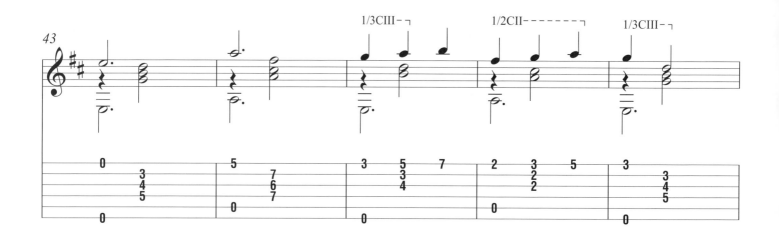
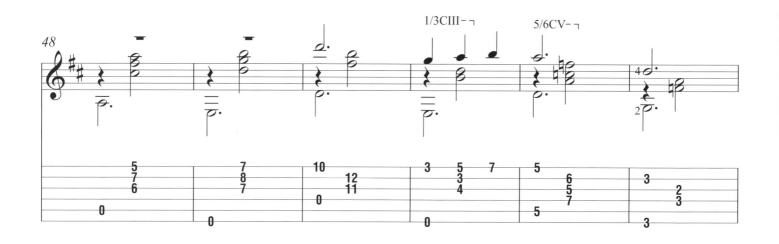
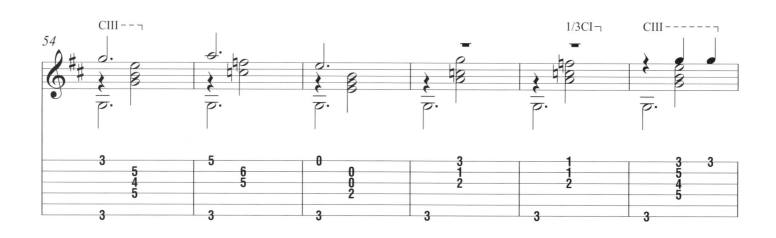
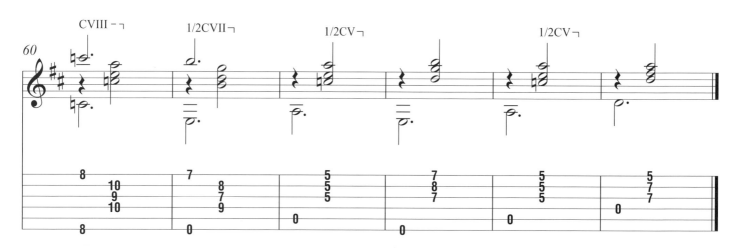

Gnossienne No. 2

Erik Satie
Arranged by Bridget Mermikides

Tuning:
(low to high) D-G-D-G-B-E

♩= ca. 53

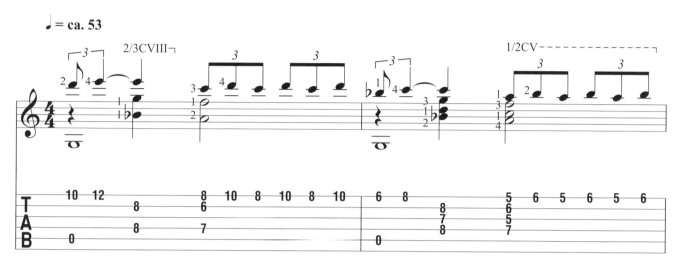

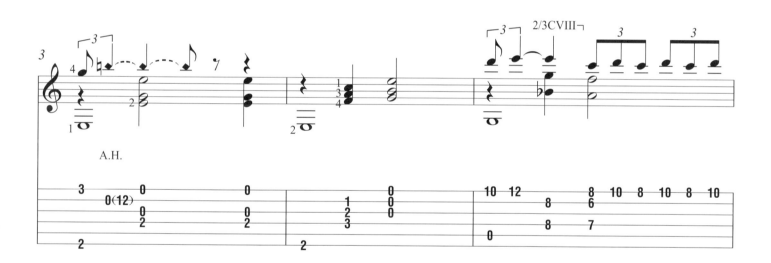

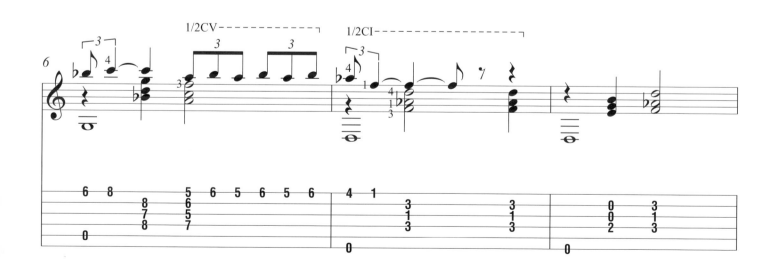

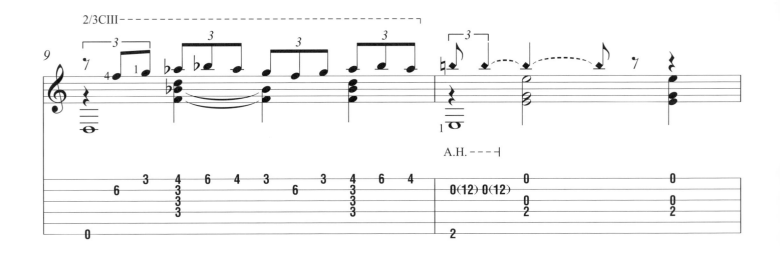

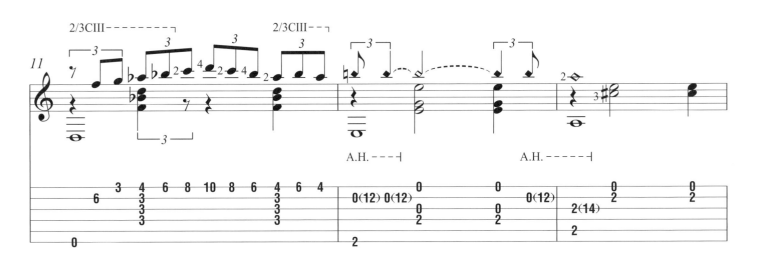

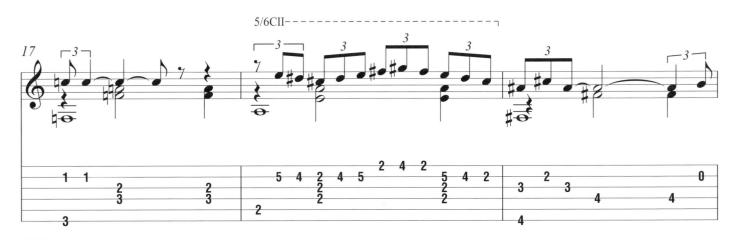

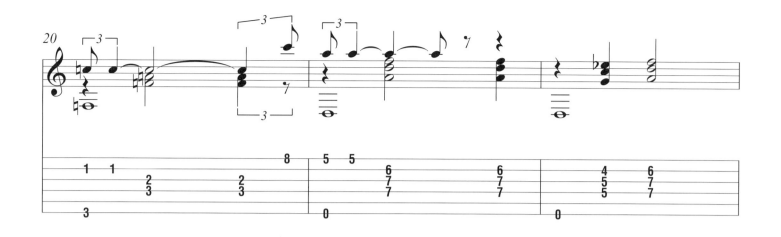
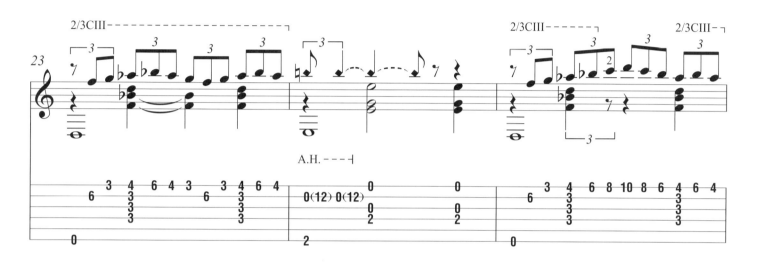
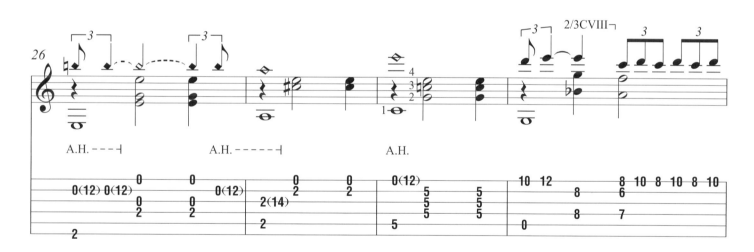

Gnossienne No. 3

Erik Satie

Arranged by Bridget Mermikides

Drop D tuning:
(low to high) D-A-D-G-B-E

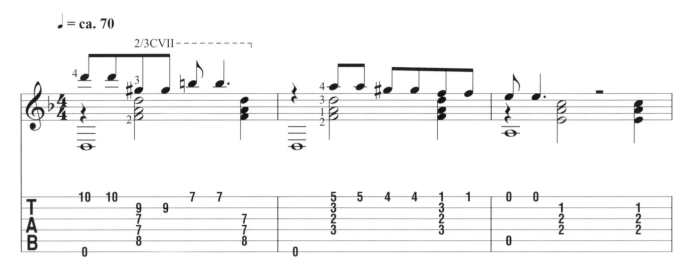

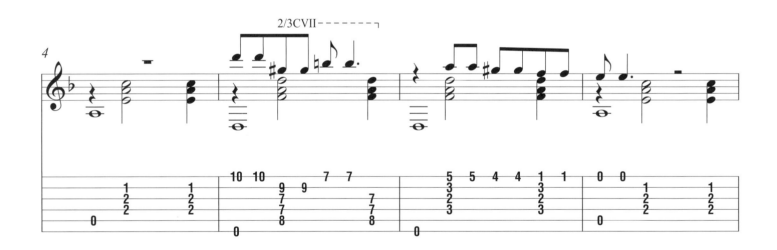

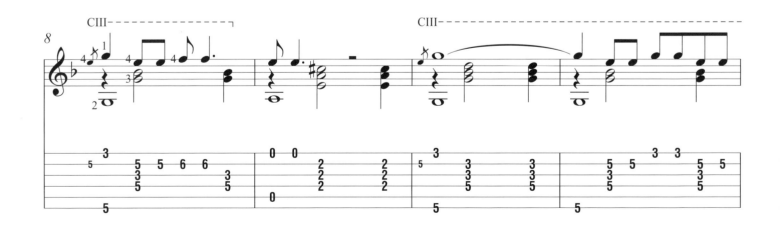

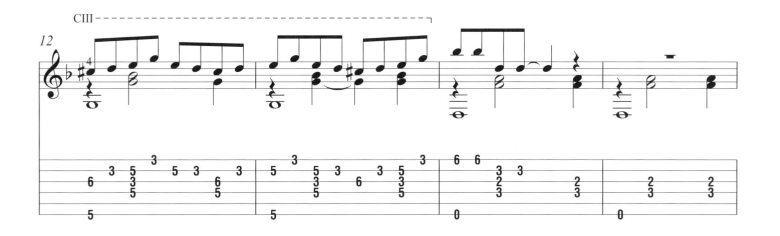

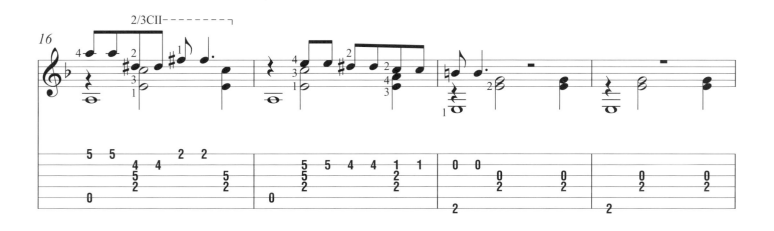

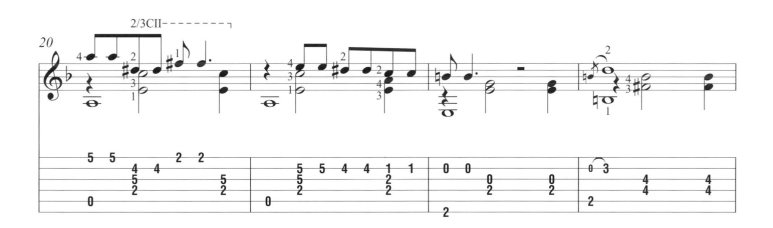

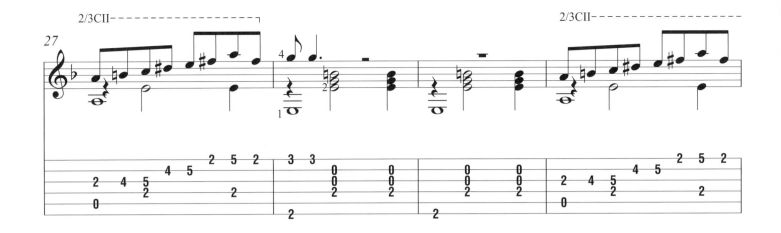

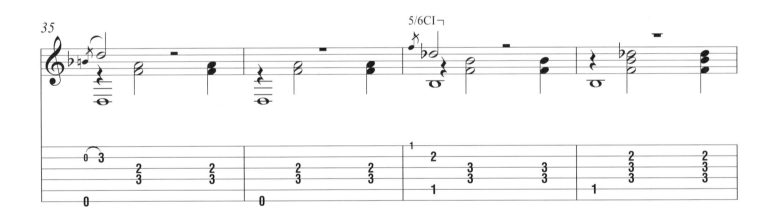

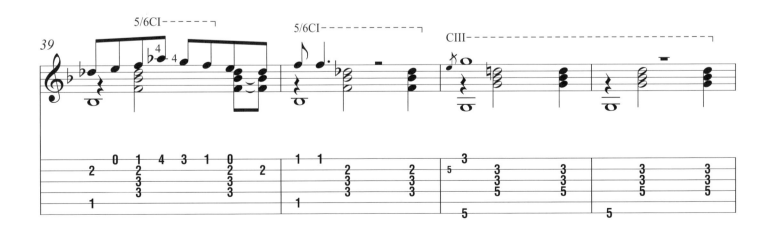

Blue Danube Waltz

Johann Strauss
Arranged by Bridget Mermikides

Drop D tuning:
(low to high) D-A-D-G-B-E

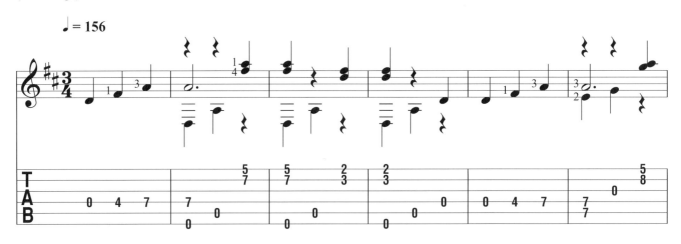

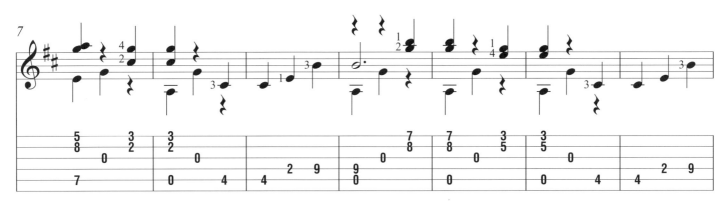

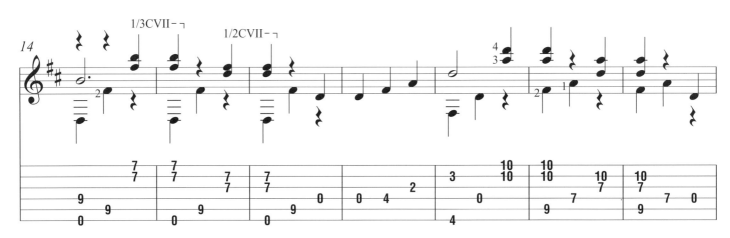

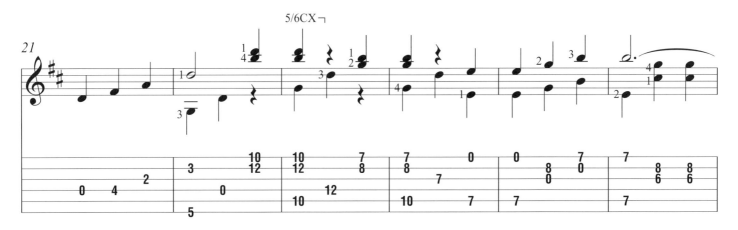

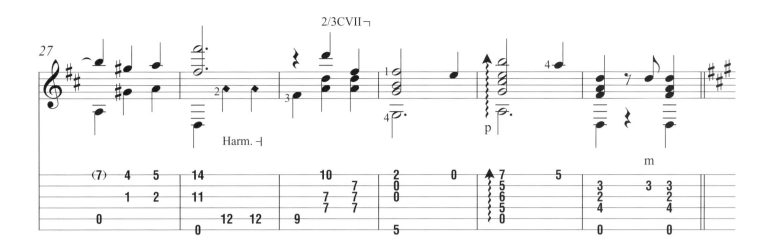

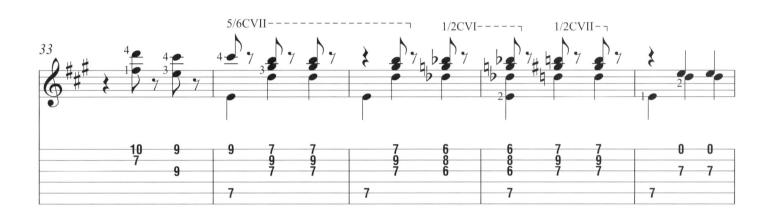

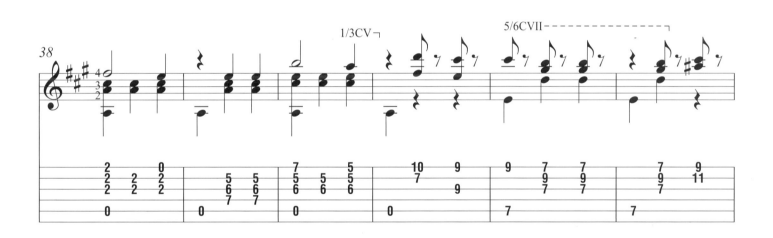

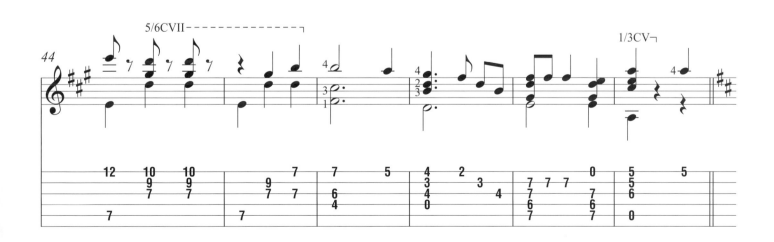

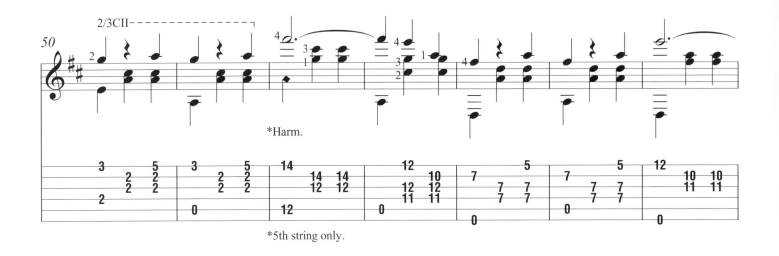

*Harm.

*5th string only.

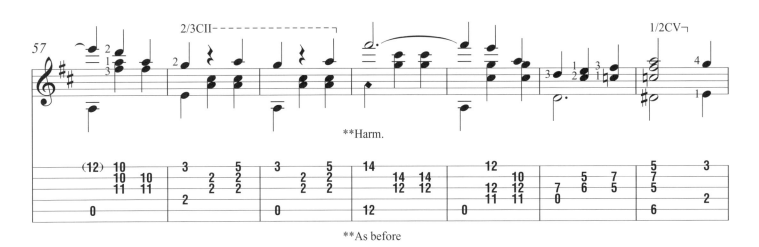

**Harm.

**As before

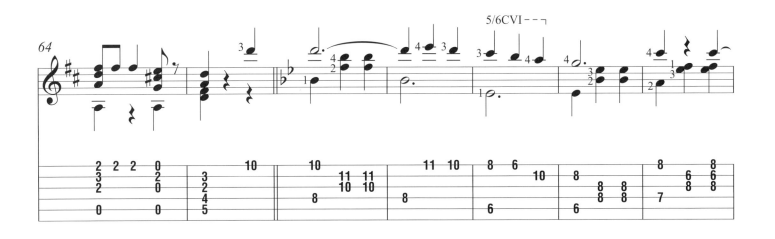

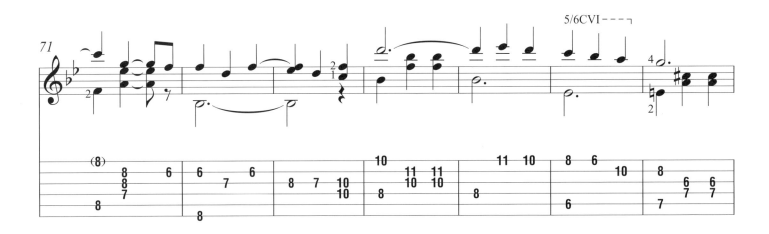

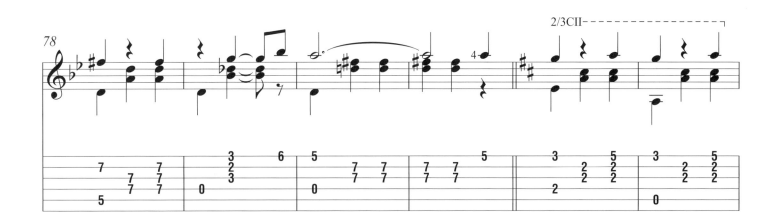

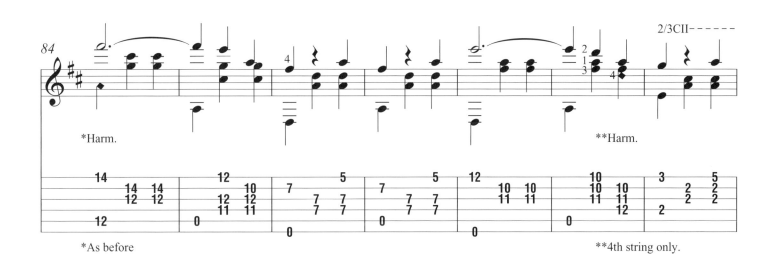

*Harm.

*As before

**Harm.

**4th string only.

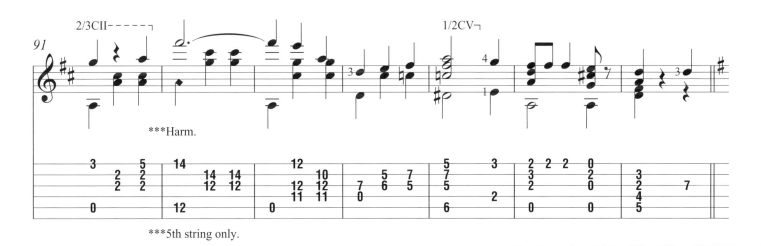

***Harm.

***5th string only.

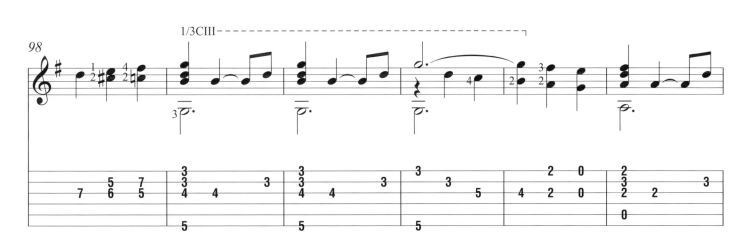

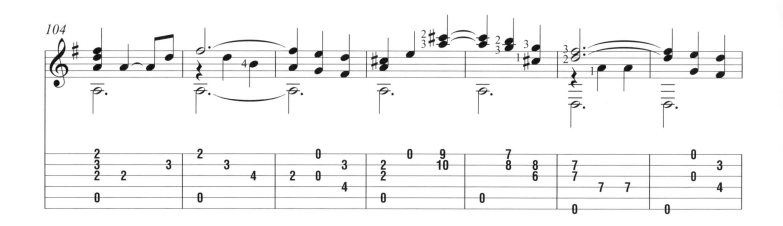

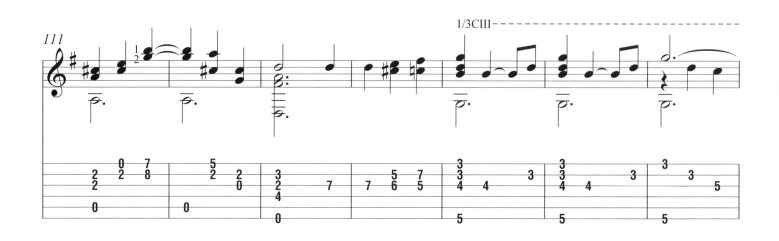

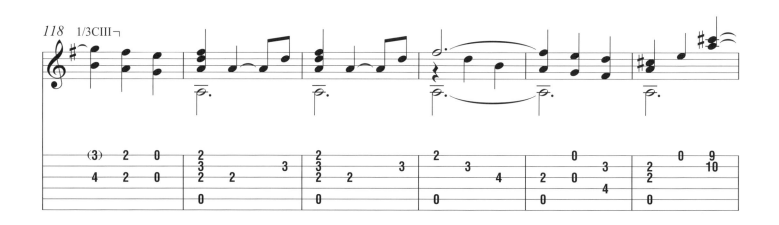

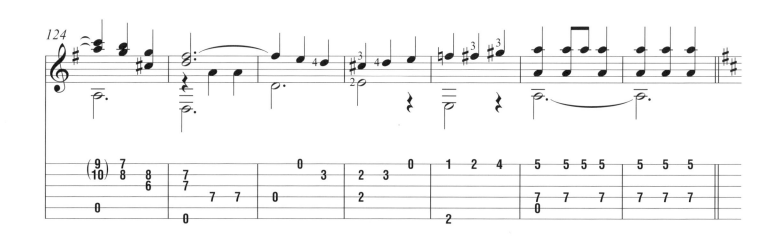

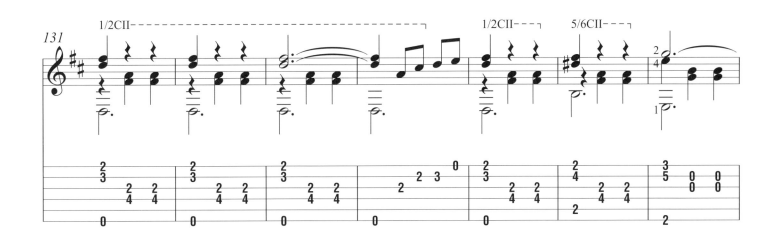

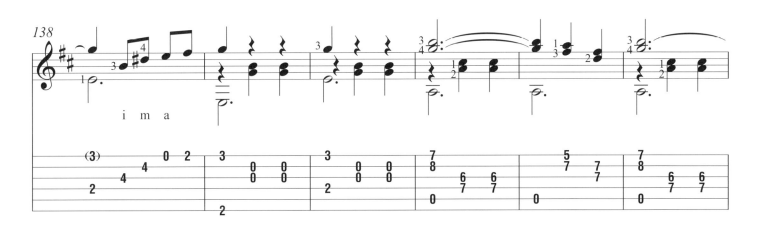

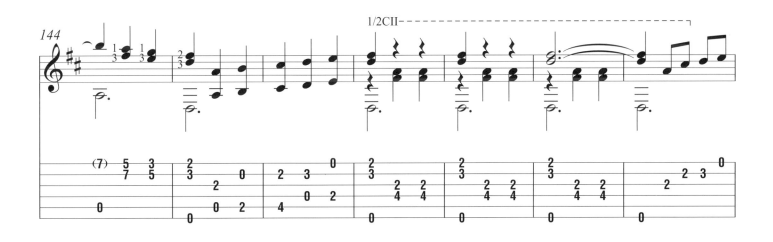

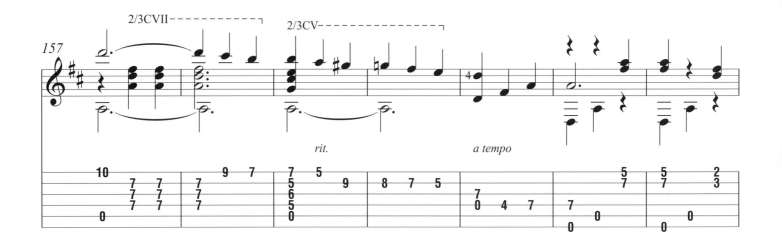

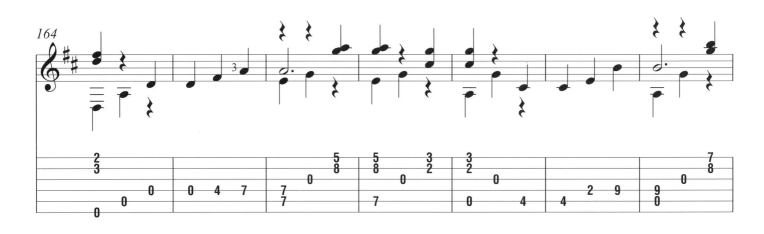

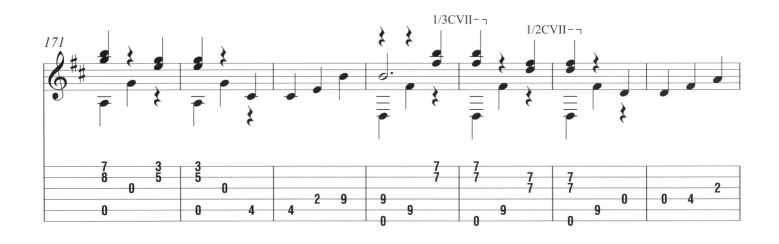

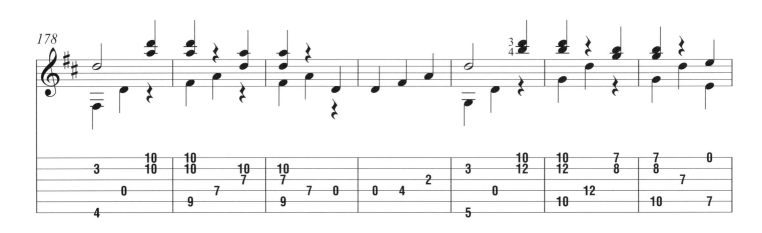

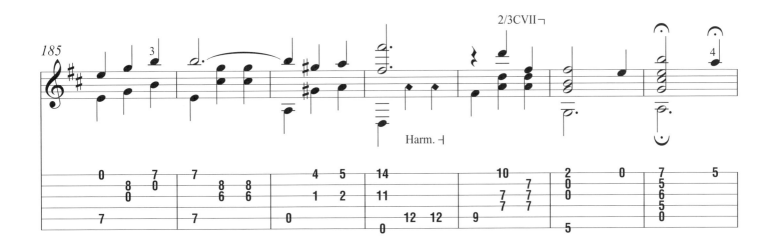

Vienna Blood Waltz

Johann Strauss II
Arranged by Bridget Mermikides

Drop D tuning:
(low to high) D-A-D-G-B-E

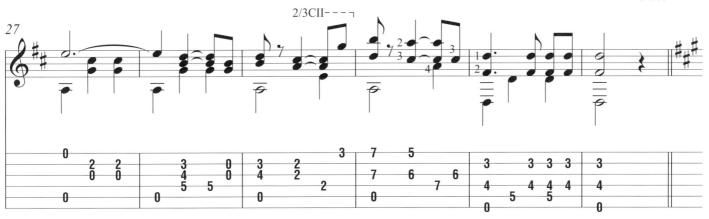

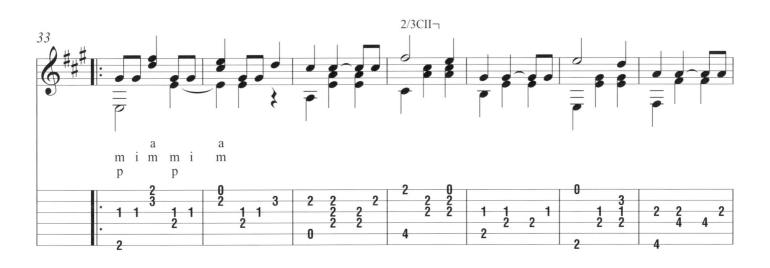

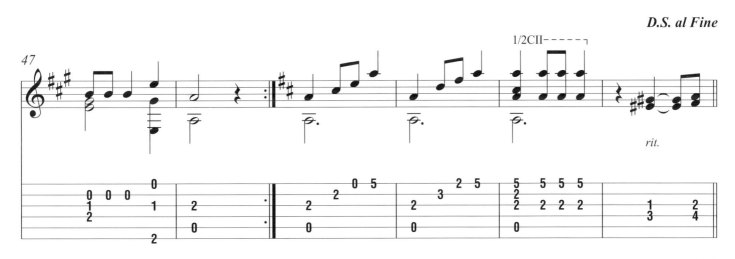

Radetzky March

Johann Strauss
Arranged by Bridget Mermikides

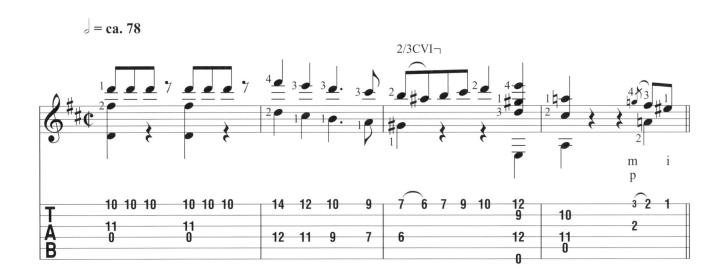

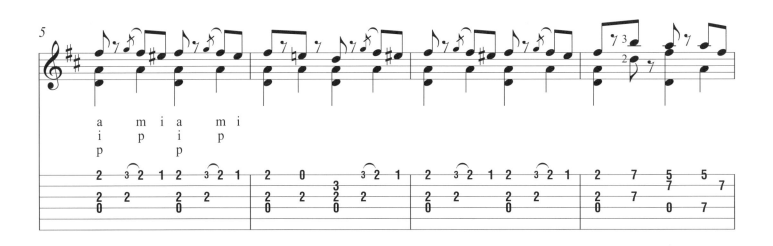

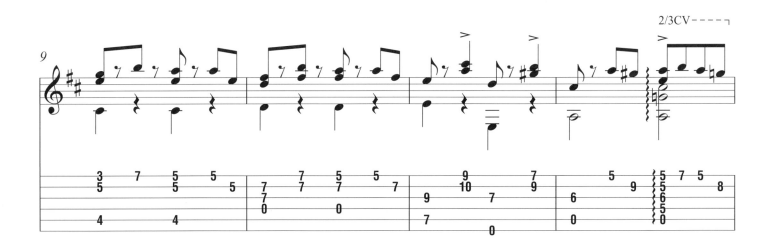

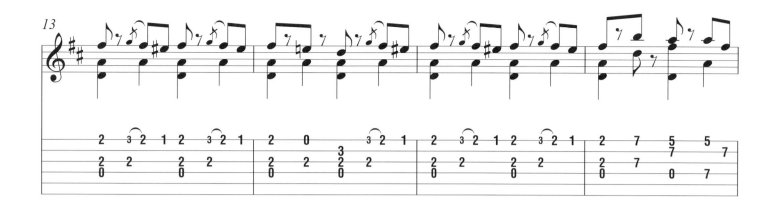

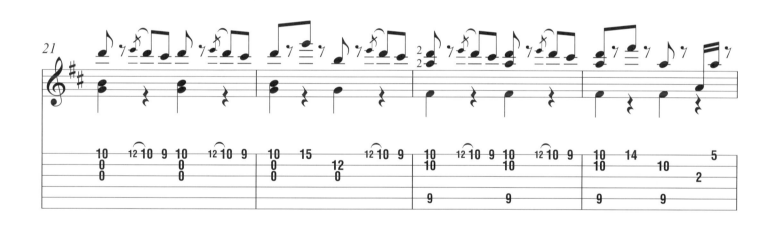
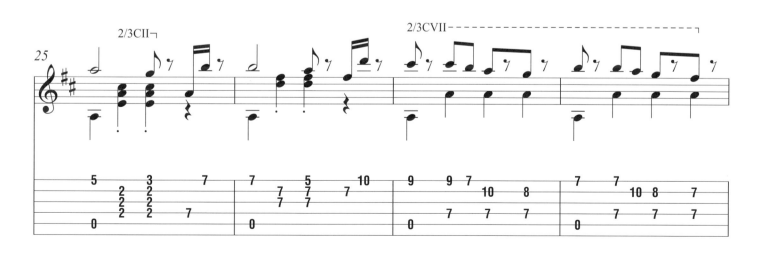

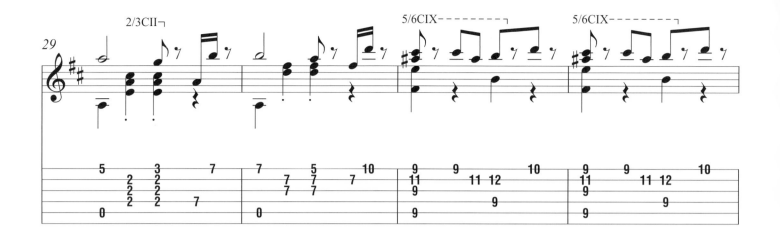

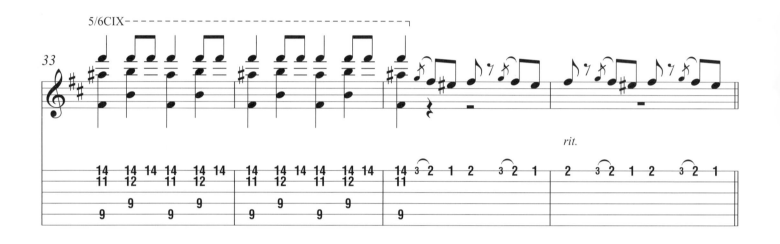

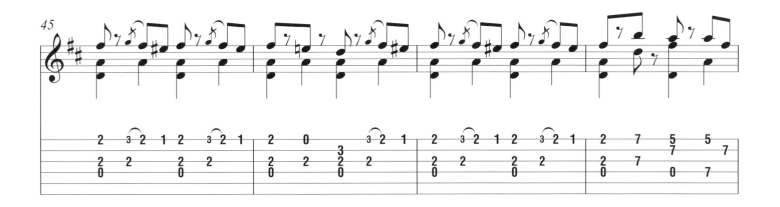

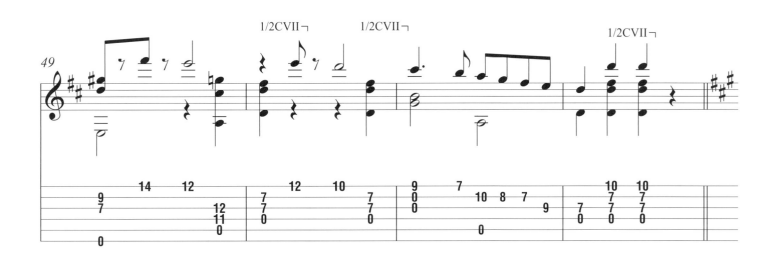

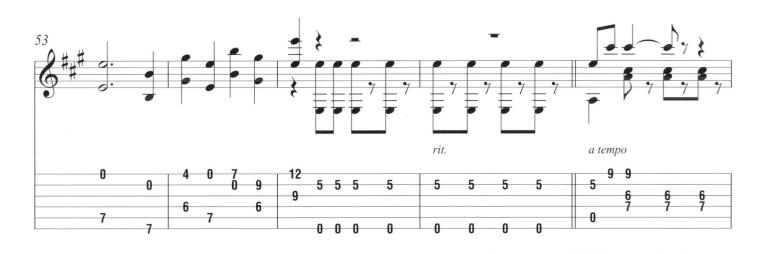

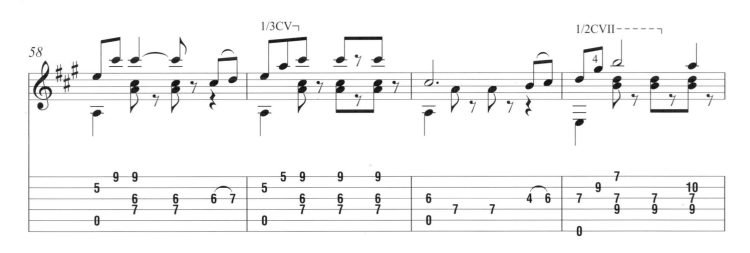

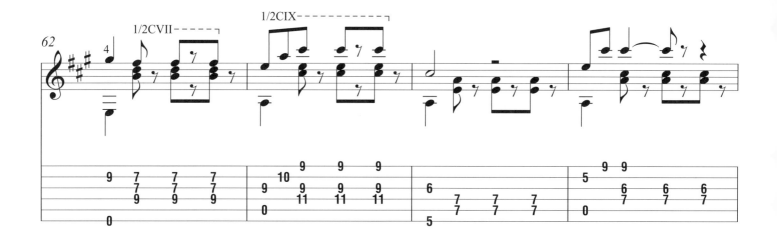

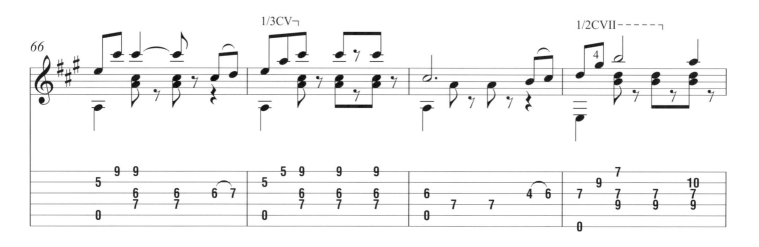

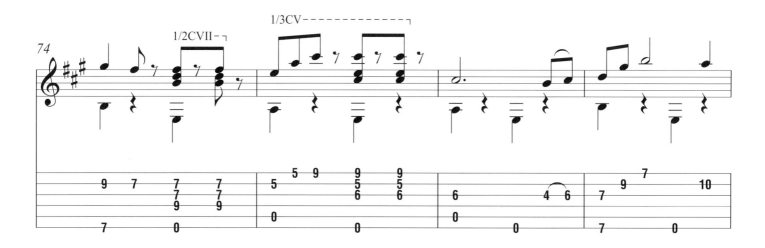

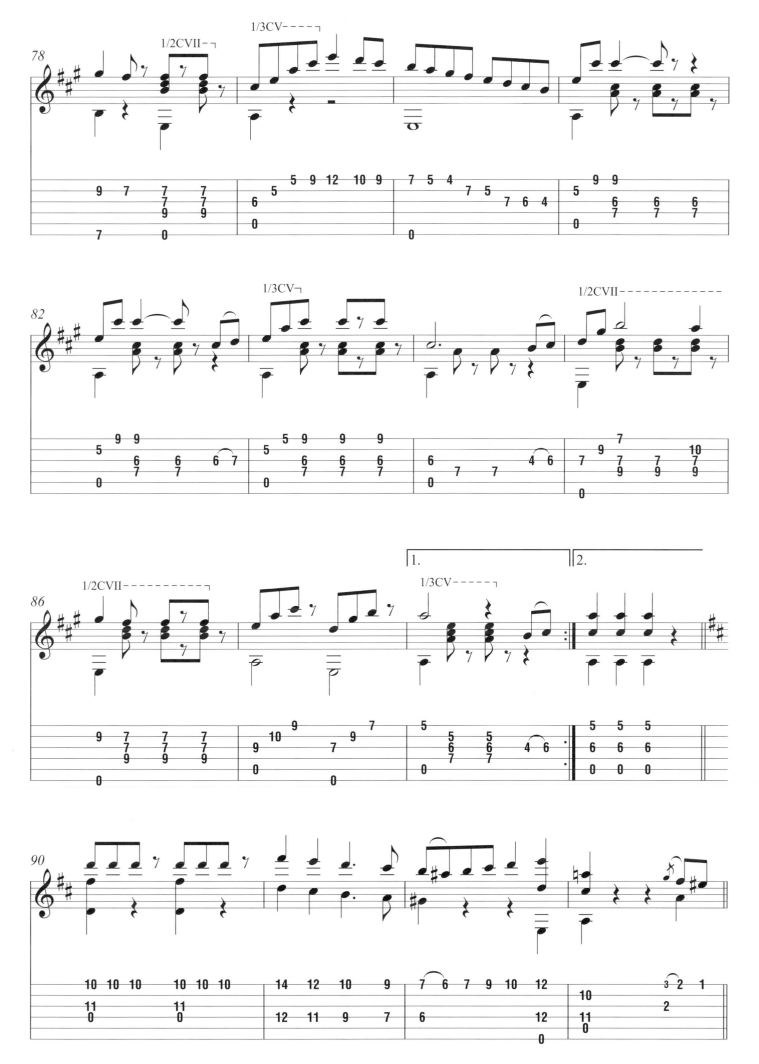

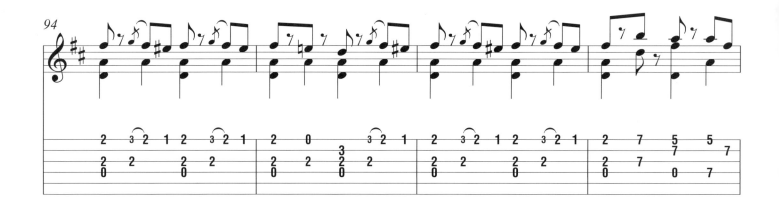

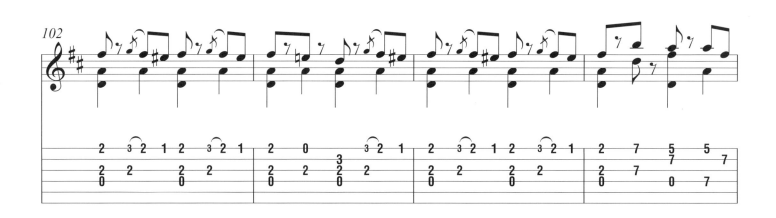

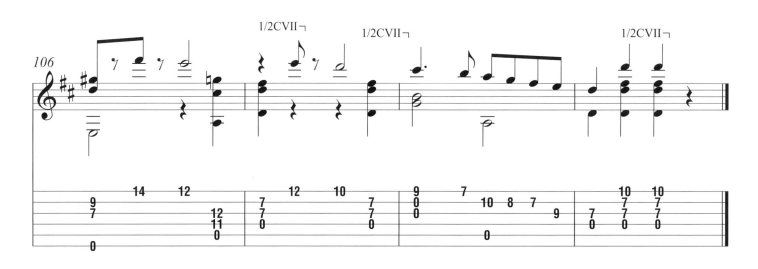

Gran Vals

Francisco Tárrega
Arranged by Bridget Mermikides

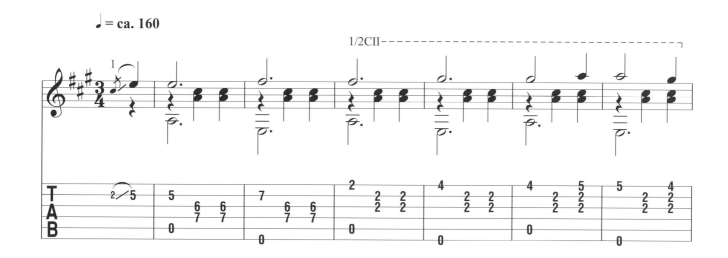

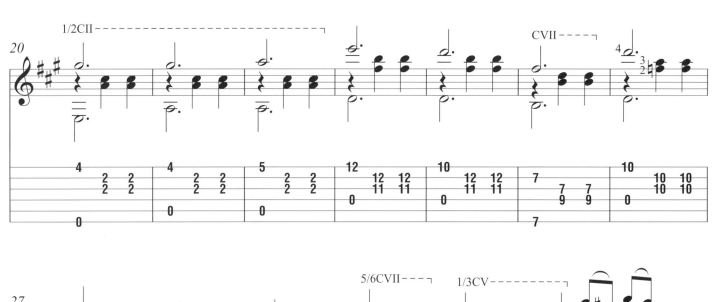

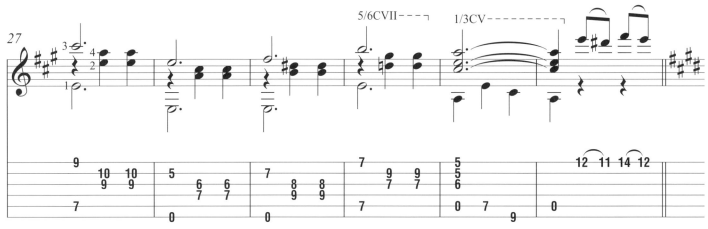

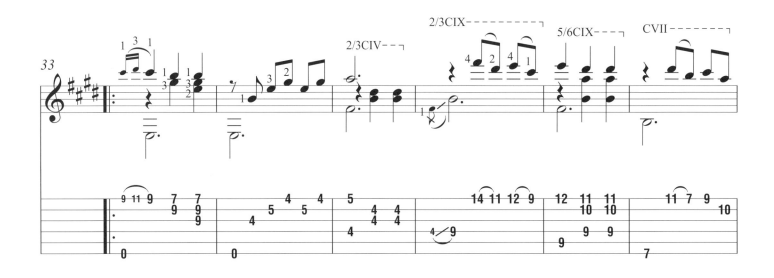

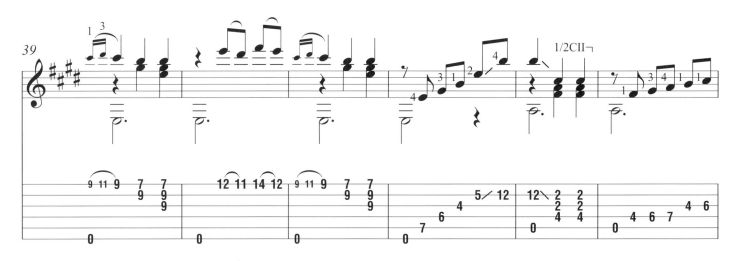

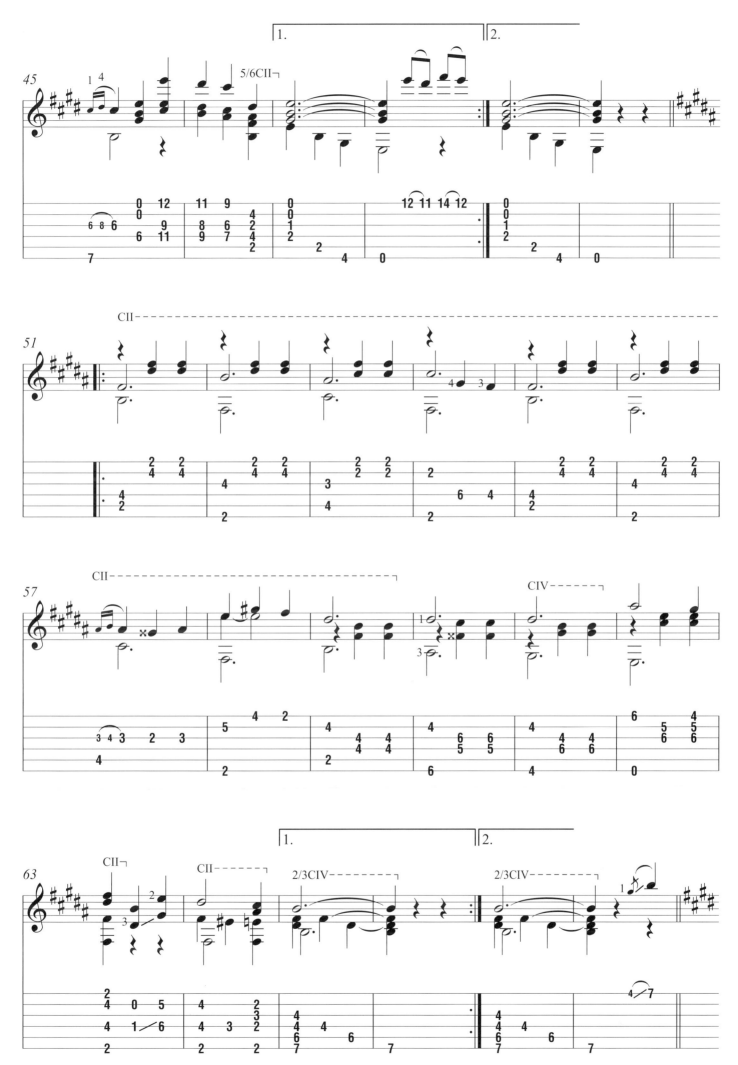

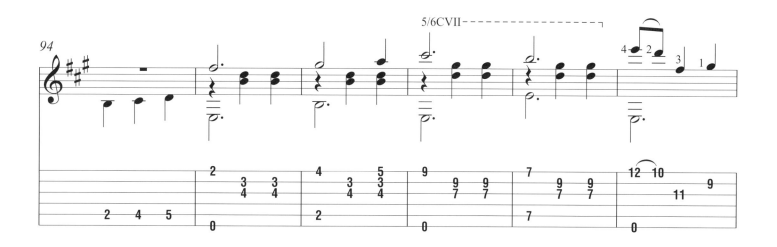

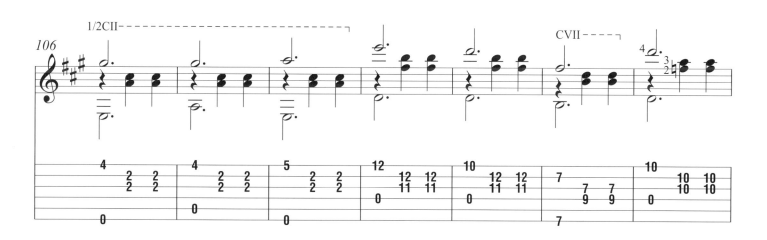

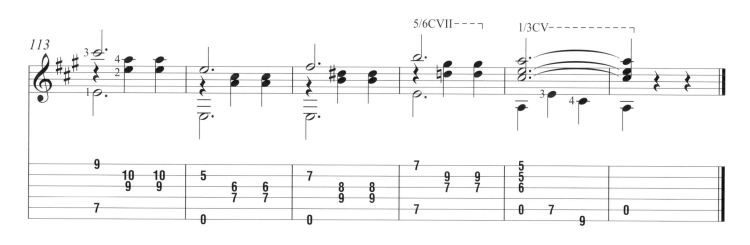

Recuerdos de la Alhambra

Francisco Tárrega
Arranged by Bridget Mermikides

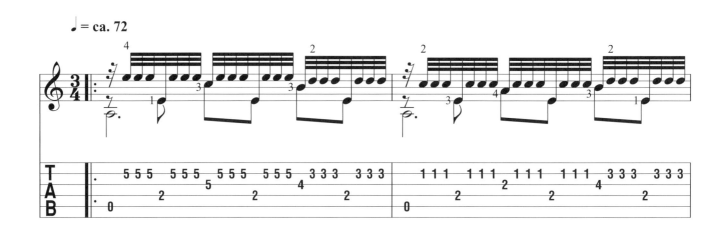

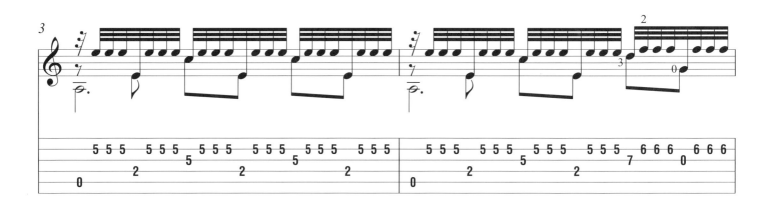

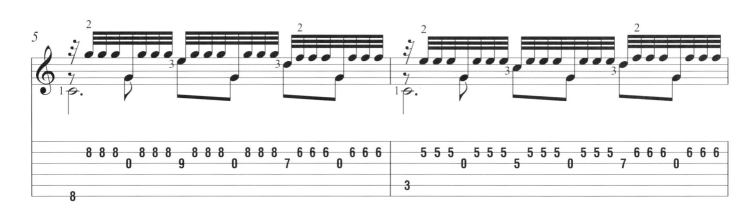

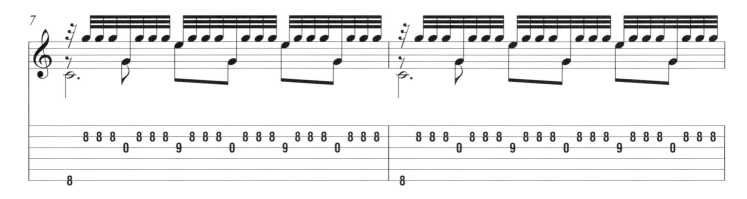

*w/ base segment of finger

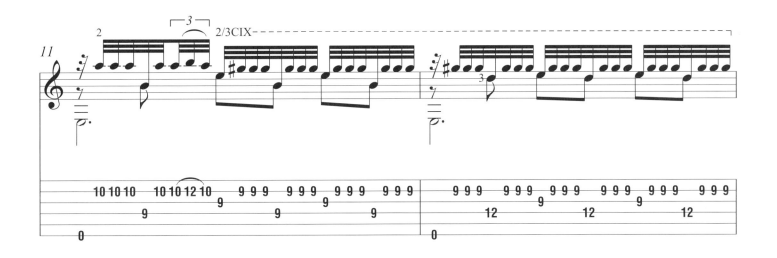

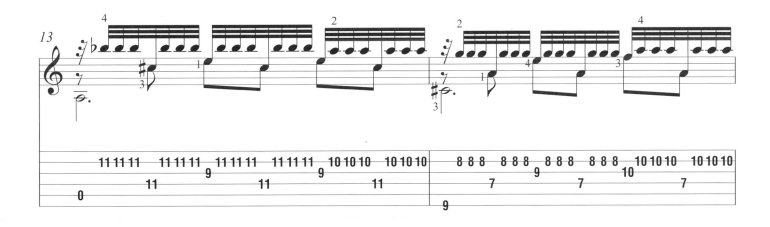

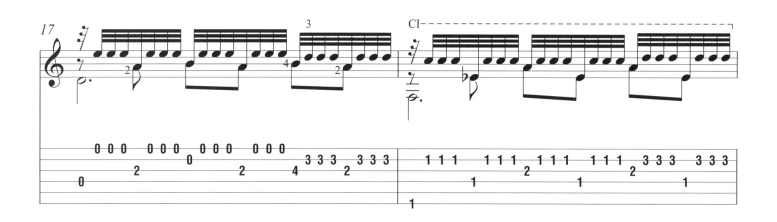

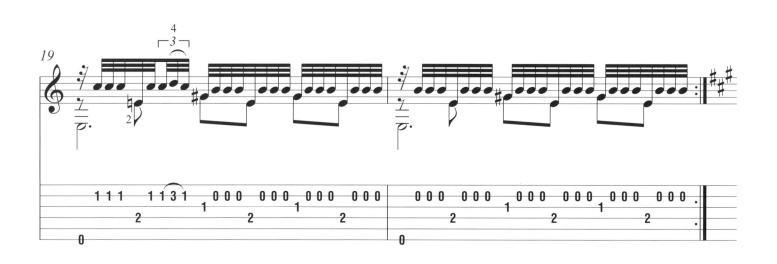

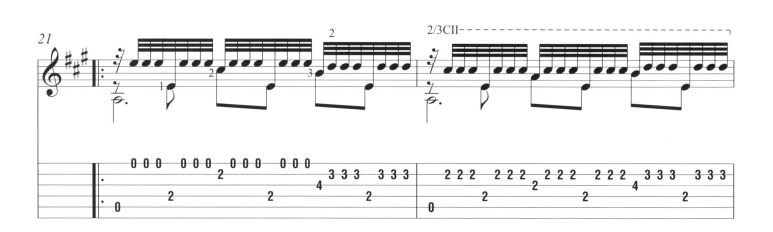

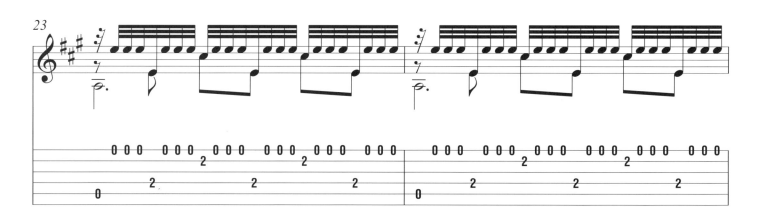

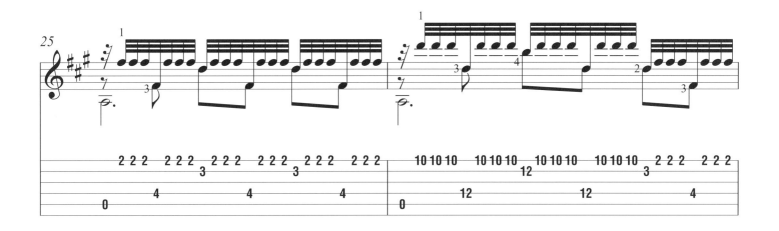

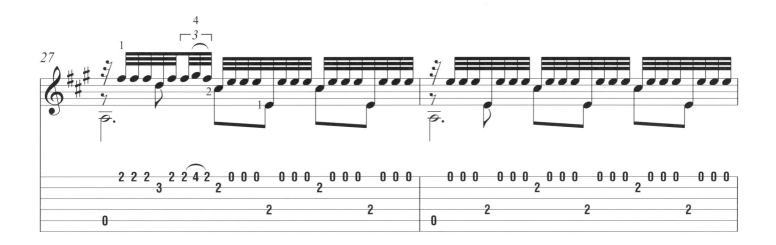

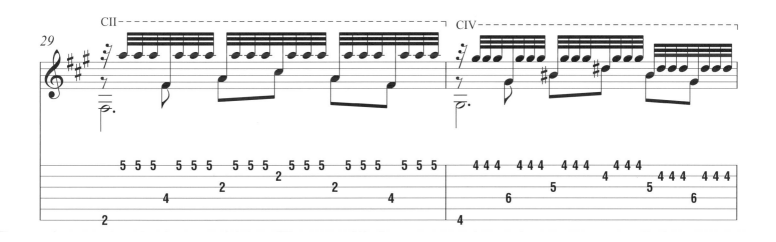

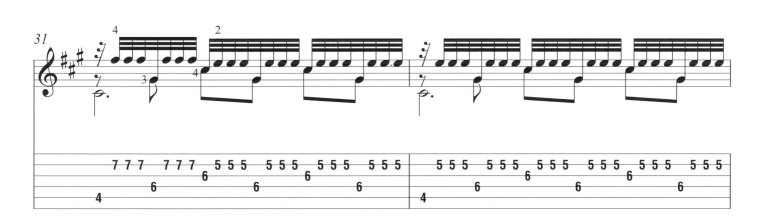

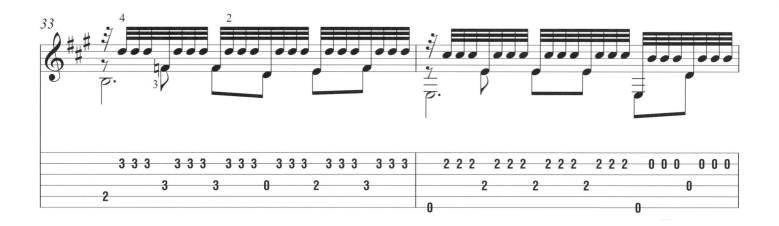

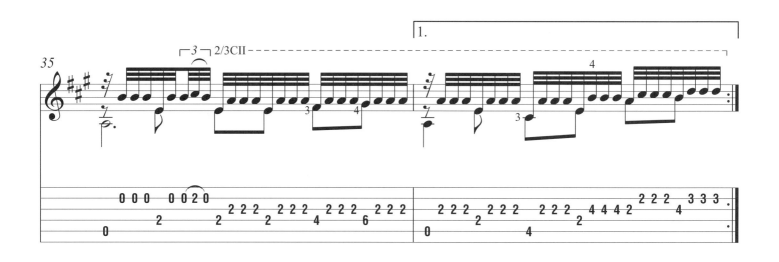

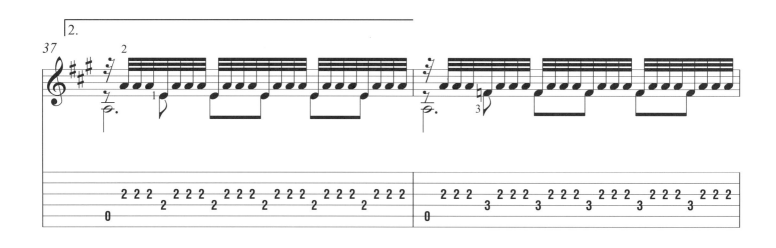

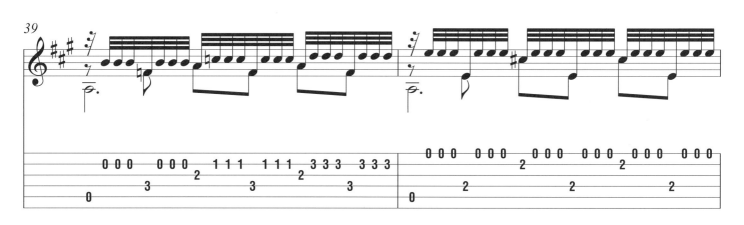

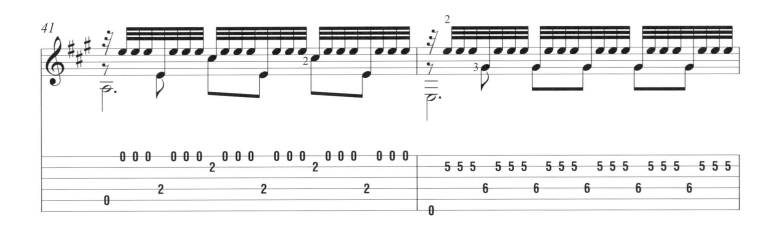

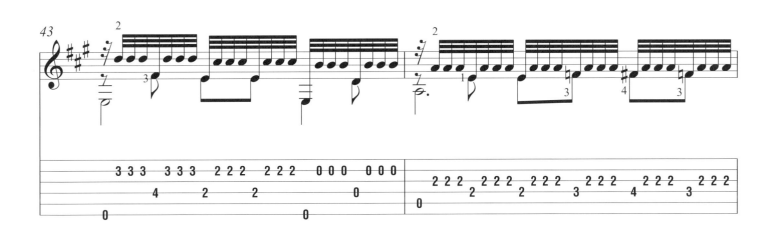

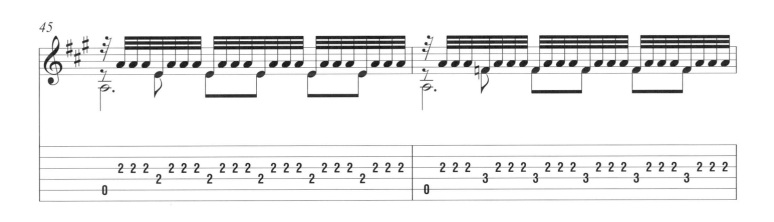

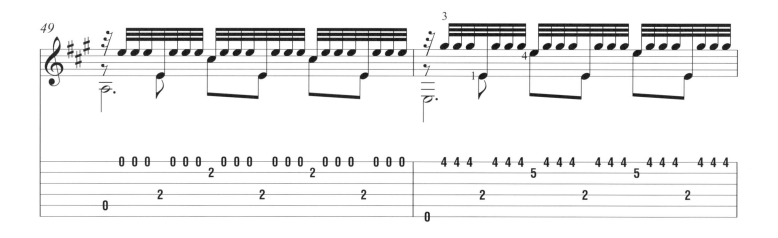

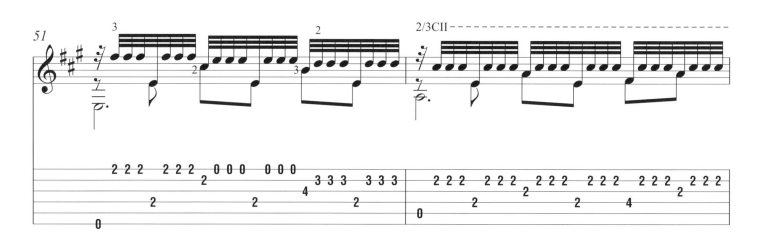

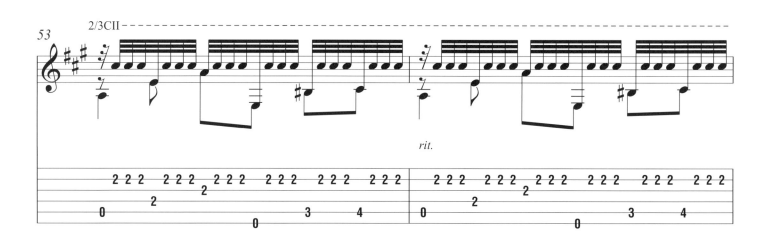

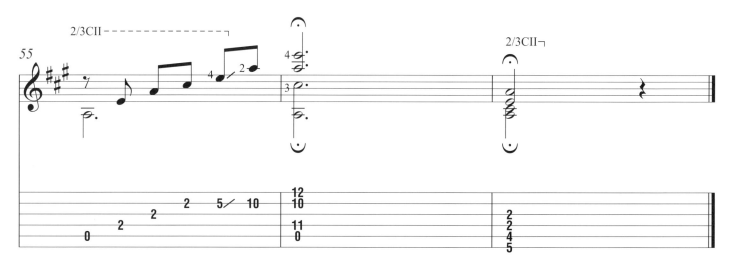

Theme from Swan Lake

Pyotr Ilyich Tchaikovsky
Arranged by Bridget Mermikides

♩ = ca. 75

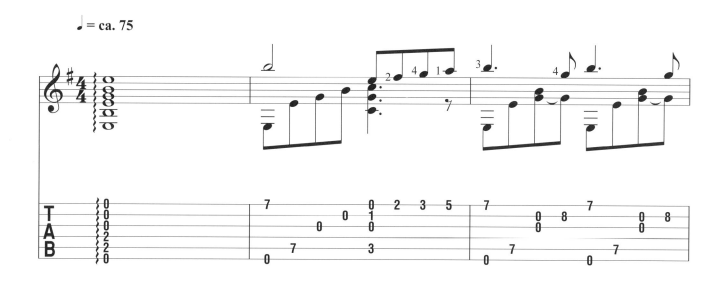

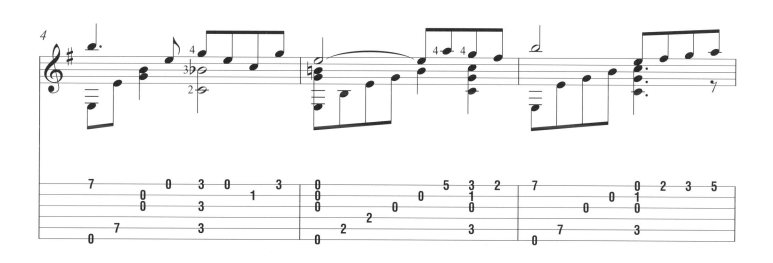

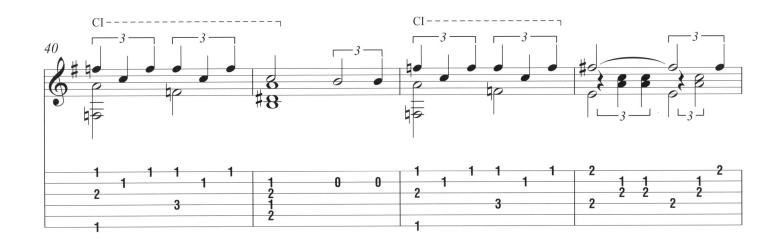

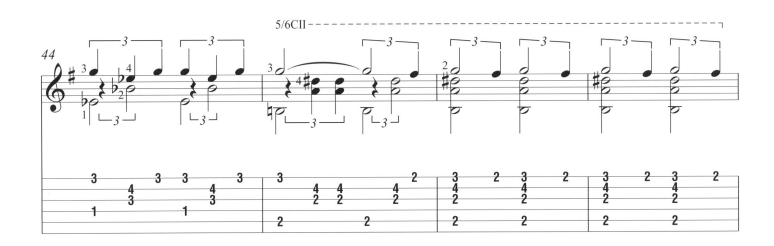

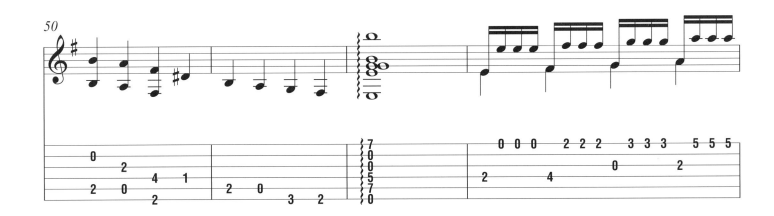

La Donna e Mobile

Giuseppe Verdi

Arranged by Bridget Mermikides

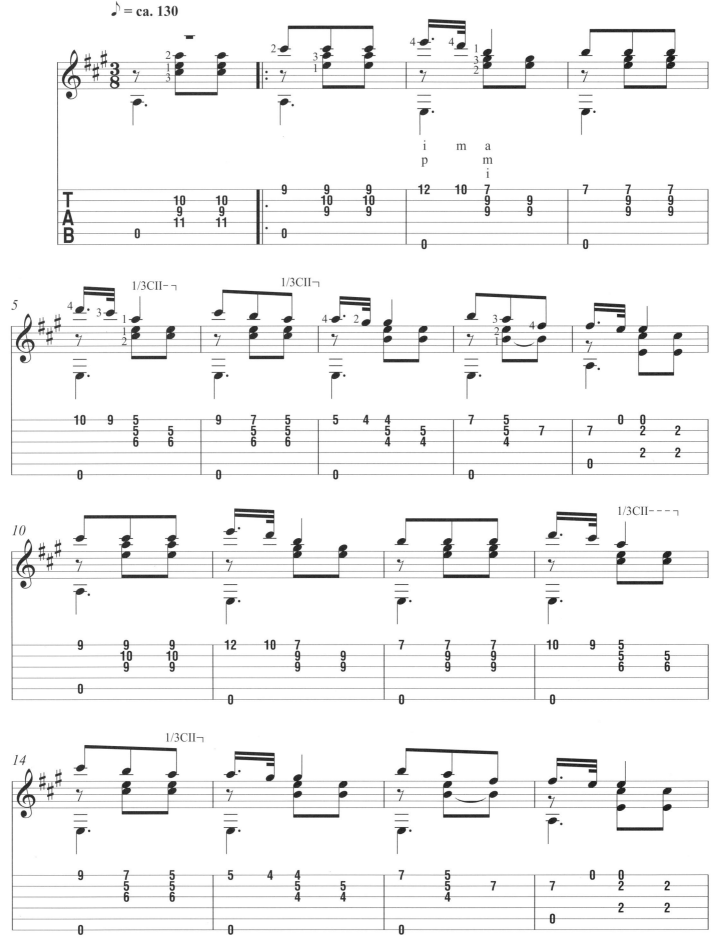

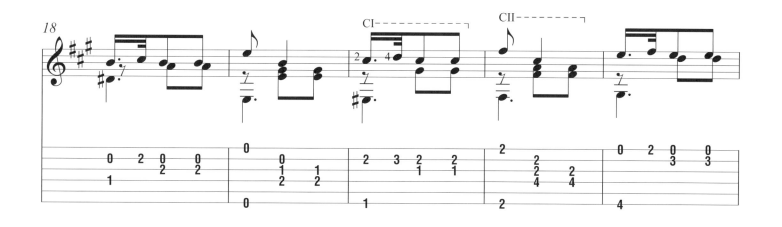

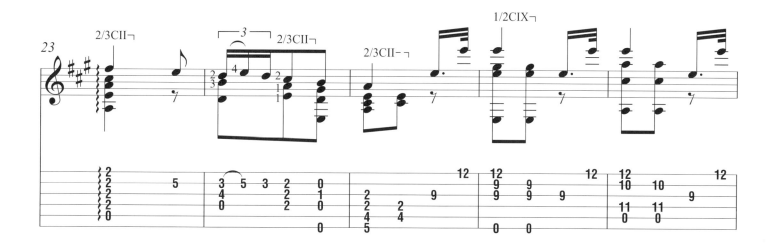

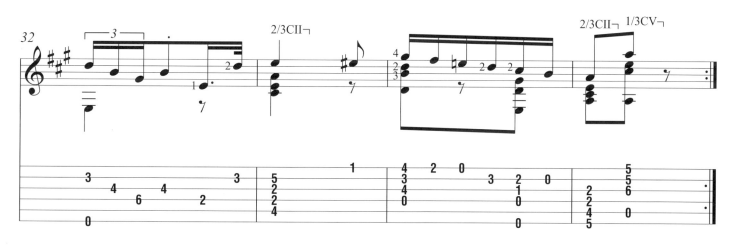

Largo from Winter - 4 Seasons

Antonio Vivaldi
Arranged by Bridget Mermikides

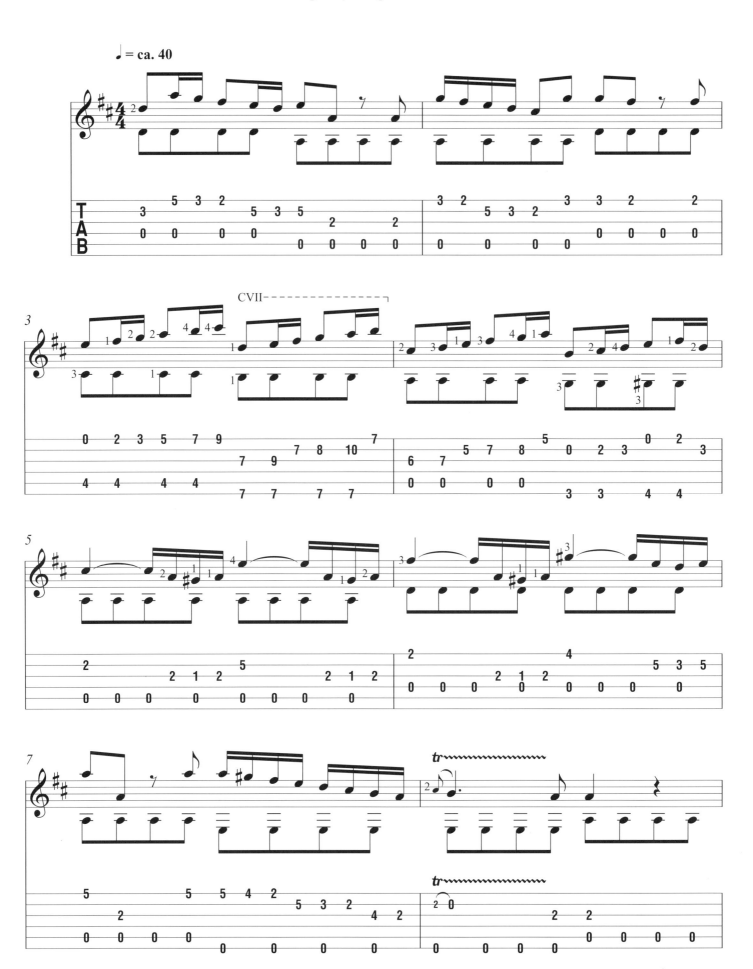

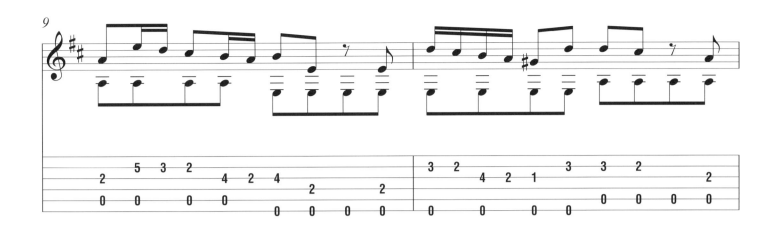

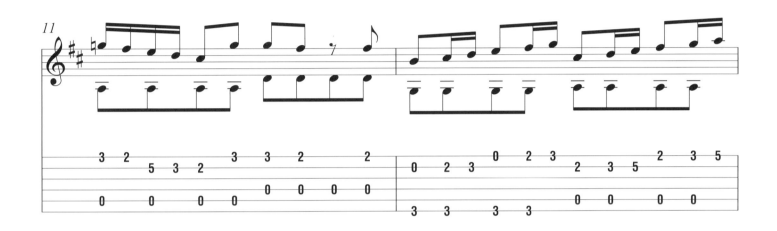

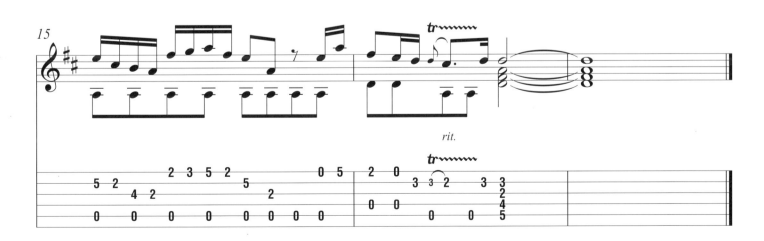

Waltz of the Flowers

Pyotr Ilyich Tchaikovsky
Arranged by Bridget Mermikides

Drop D tuning:
(low to high) D-A-D-G-B-E

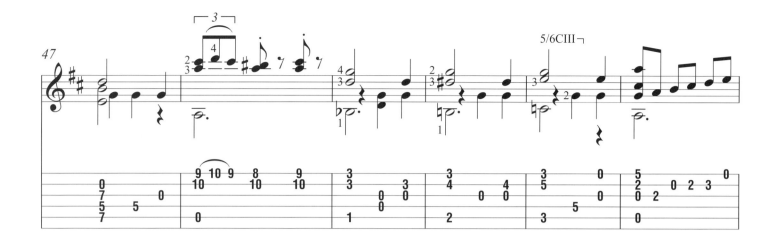

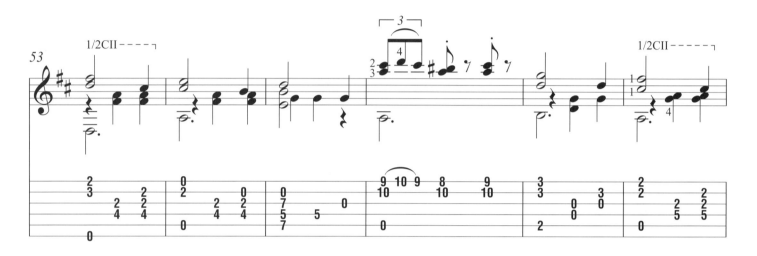

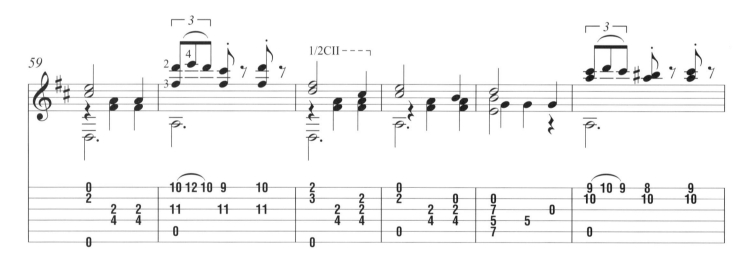

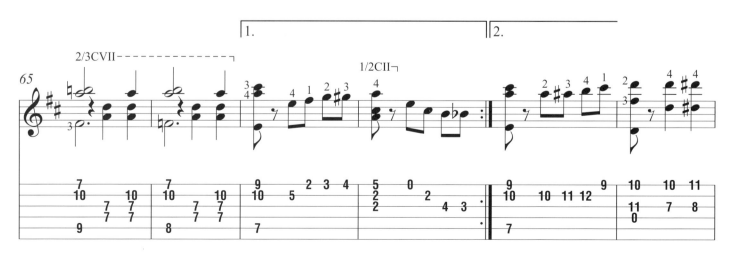

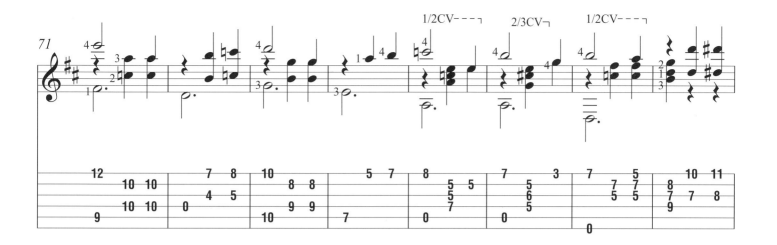
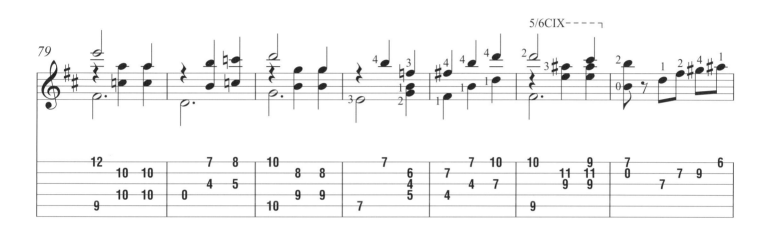

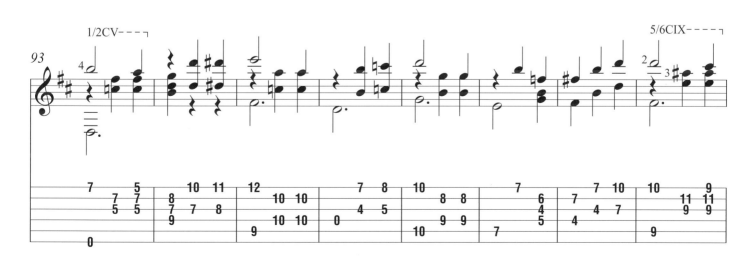

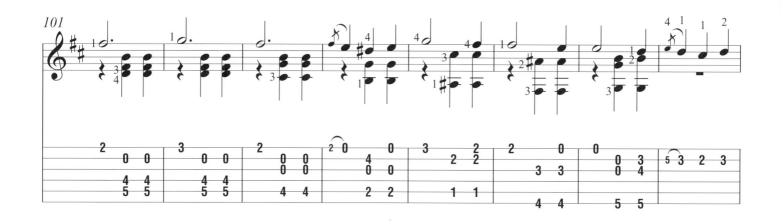

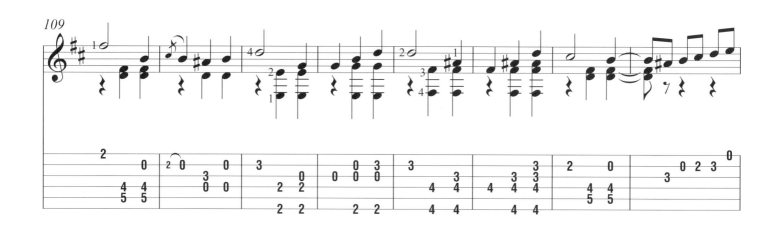

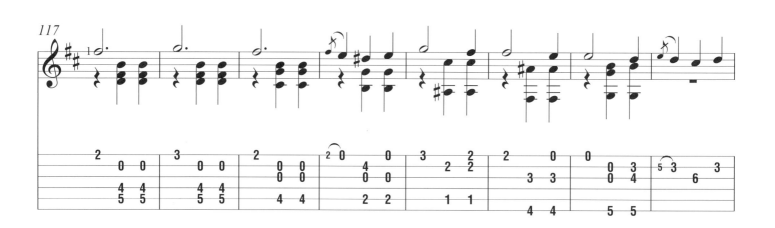

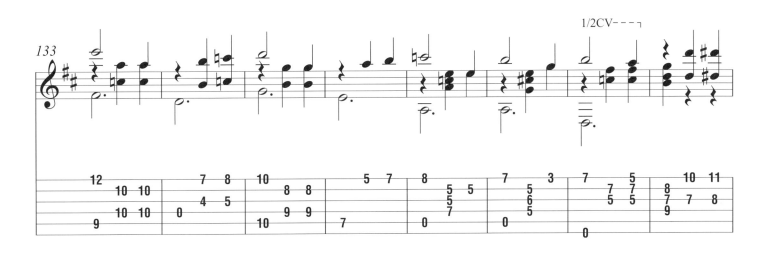

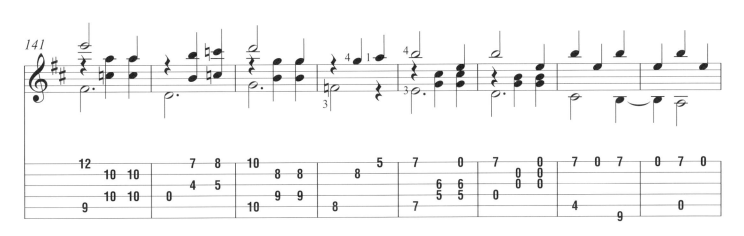

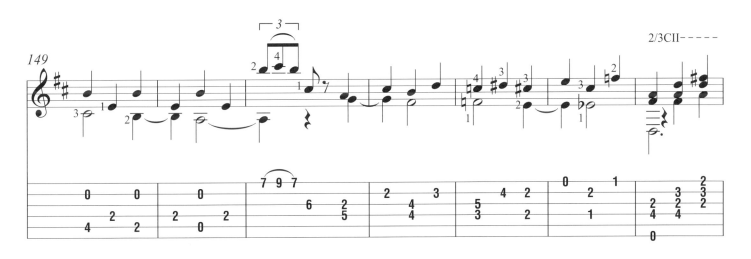

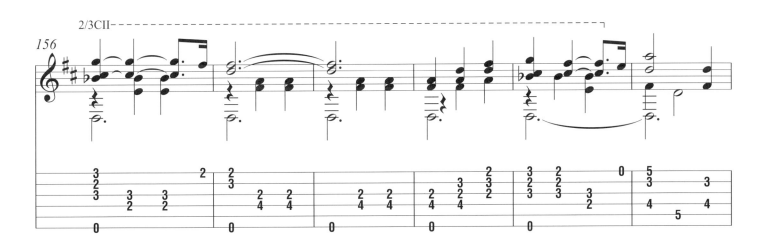

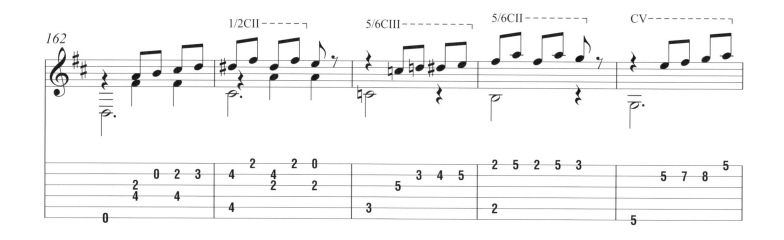

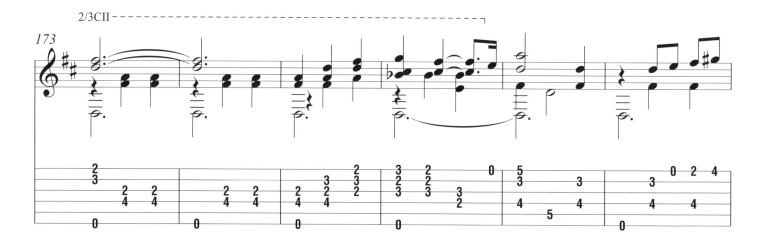

About the Author

Bridget Mermikides (formerly Upson) grew up in a family of classical musicians in the Lake District of England and studied the cello at age 6. Upon hearing a John Williams recording at age 13, she became instantly and irrecoverably smitten with the classical guitar and has since devoted her life to the instrument.

A graduate of the Royal Academy of Music (where she received tuition from John Williams and Julian Bream), Bridget now teaches, performs as a soloist and ensemble player and writes a monthly classical guitar column for *Guitar Techniques* magazine. Bridget lives in London with her husband and daughter.

www.bridgetmermikides.com

CLASSICAL GUITAR

THE BEATLES FOR CLASSICAL GUITAR

Includes 20 solos from big Beatles hits arranged for classical guitar, complete with left-hand and right-hand fingering. Songs include: All My Loving • And I Love Her • Can't Buy Me Love • Fool on the Hill • From a Window • Hey Jude • If I Fell • Let It Be • Michelle • Norwegian Wood • Obla Di • Ticket to Ride • Yesterday • and more. Features arrangements and an introduction by Joe Washington, as well as his helpful hints on classical technique and detailed notes on how to play each song. The book also covers parts and specifications of the classical guitar, tuning, and Joe's "Strata System" – an easy-reading system applied to chord diagrams.
00699237 Classical Guitar $19.99

CZERNY FOR GUITAR

INCLUDES TAB

12 SCALE STUDIES FOR CLASSICAL GUITAR
by David Patterson

Adapted from Carl Czerny's *School of Velocity, Op. 299* for piano, this lesson book explores 12 keys with 12 different approaches or "treatments." You will explore a variety of articulations, ranges and technical perspectives as you learn each key. These arrangements will not only improve your ability to play scales fluently, but will also develop your ears, knowledge of the fingerboard, reading abilities, strength and endurance. In standard notation and tablature.
00701248 ....$9.99

MATTEO CARCASSI – 25 MELODIC AND PROGRESSIVE STUDIES, OP. 60

arr. Paul Henry

One of Carcassi's (1792-1853) most famous collections of classical guitar music – indispensable for the modern guitarist's musical and technical development. Performed by Paul Henry. 49-minute audio accompaniment.
00696506 Book/Online Audio $17.99

CLASSICAL & FINGERSTYLE GUITAR TECHNIQUES

INCLUDES TAB

by David Oakes • Musicians Institute

This Master Class is aimed at any electric or acoustic guitarist who wants a quick, thorough grounding in the essentials of classical and fingerstyle technique. Topics covered include: arpeggios and scales, free stroke and rest stroke, P-i scale technique, three-to-a-string patterns, natural and artificial harmonics, tremolo and rasgueado, and more. The book includes 12 intensive lessons for right and left hand in standard notation & tab, and the audio features 92 solo acoustic tracks.
00695171 Book/Online Audio $17.99

CLASSICAL GUITAR CHRISTMAS COLLECTION

INCLUDES TAB

Includes classical guitar arrangements in standard notation and tablature for more than two dozen beloved carols: Angels We Have Heard on High • Auld Lang Syne • Ave Maria • Away in a Manger • Canon in D • The First Noel • God Rest Ye Merry, Gentlemen • Hark! the Herald Angels Sing • I Saw Three Ships • Jesu, Joy of Man's Desiring • Joy to the World • O Christmas Tree • O Holy Night • Silent Night • What Child Is This? • and more.
00699493 Guitar Solo $10.99

CLASSICAL GUITAR WEDDING

INCLUDES TAB

Perfect for players hired to perform for someone's big day, this songbook features 16 classsical wedding favorites arranged for solo guitar in standard notation and tablature. Includes: Air on the G String • Ave Maria • Bridal Chorus • Canon in D • Jesu, Joy of Man's Desiring • Minuet • Sheep May Safely Graze • Wedding March • and more.
00699563 Solo Guitar with Tab.............................$12.99

CLASSICAL MASTERPIECES FOR GUITAR

INCLUDES TAB

27 works by Bach, Beethoven, Handel, Mendelssohn, Mozart and more transcribed with standard notation and tablature. Now anyone can enjoy classical material regardless of their guitar background. Also features stay-open binding.
00699312 ....$14.99

MASTERWORKS FOR GUITAR

INCLUDES TAB

Over 60 Favorites from Four Centuries
World's Great Classical Music

Dozens of classical masterpieces: Allemande • Bourree • Canon in D • Jesu, Joy of Man's Desiring • Lagrima • Malaguena • Mazurka • Piano Sonata No. 14 in C# Minor (Moonlight) Op. 27 No. 2 First Movement Theme • Ode to Joy • Prelude No. I (Well-Tempered Clavier).
00699503 ....$19.99

HAL•LEONARD®

Visit Hal Leonard Online at **www.halleonard.com**

Prices, contents and availability subject to change without notice.

A MODERN APPROACH TO CLASSICAL GUITAR

by Charles Duncan

This multi-volume method was developed to allow students to study the art of classical guitar within a new, more contemporary framework. For private, class or self-instruction. Book One incorporates chord frames and symbols, as well as a recording to assist in tuning and to provide accompaniments for at-home practice. Book One also introduces beginning fingerboard technique and music theory. Book Two and Three build upon the techniques learned in Book One.
00695114 Book 1 – Book Only $6.99
00695113 Book 1 – Book/Online Audio................$10.99
00695116 Book 2 – Book Only $6.99
00695115 Book 2 – Book/Online Audio................$10.99
00699202 Book 3 – Book Only $9.99
00695117 Book 3 – Book/Online Audio................$12.99
00695119 Composite Book/CD Pack.....................$29.99

ANDRES SEGOVIA – 20 STUDIES FOR GUITAR

Sor/Segovia

20 studies for the classical guitar written by Beethoven's contemporary, Fernando Sor, revised, edited and fingered by the great classical guitarist Andres Segovia. These essential repertoire pieces continue to be used by teachers and students to build solid classical technique. Features 50-minute demonstration audio.
00695012 Book/Online Audio $19.99
00006363 Book Only..$7.99

THE FRANCISCO COLLECTION TÁRREGA

INCLUDES TAB

edited and performed by Paul Henry

Considered the father of modern classical guitar, Francisco Tárrega revolutionized guitar technique and composed a wealth of music that will be a cornerstone of classical guitar repertoire for centuries to come. This unique book/audio pack features 14 of his most outstanding pieces in standard notation and tab, edited and performed by virtuoso Paul Henry. Includes: Adelita • Capricho Árabe • Estudio Brillante • Grand Jota • Lágrima • Malagueña • María • Recuerdos de la Alhambra • Tango • and more, plus bios of Tárrega and Henry.
00698993 Book/Online Audio $19.99